WESTMAR COLLEGE

W9-BQZ-083

Truth and Credibility

THE JOHN DEWEY LECTURE—NUMBER SEVENTEEN

The John Dewey Lecture is delivered annually under the sponsership of the John Dewey Society. This book is an elaboration of the Lecture given in 1980. The intention of the series is to provide a setting where able thinkers from various sectors of our intellectual life can direct their most searching thought to problems that involve the relation of education to culture. Arrangements for the presentation and publication of the Lecture are under the direction of the John Dewey Society Commission on Lectures.

Gerald M. Reagan, *Chairperson and Editor*
The Ohio State University

Truth and Credibility
The Citizen's Dilemma

Harry S. Broudy

Longman

New York & London

TRUTH AND CREDIBILITY
The Citizen's Dilemma

Longman Inc., 19 West 44th Street, New York, N.Y. 10036
Associated companies, branches, and representatives
throughout the world.

Developmental Editor: Lane Akers
Editorial and Design Supervisor: Diane Perlmuth
Manufacturing and Production Supervisor: Robin B. Besofsky
Printing and Binding: Bookcrafters, Inc.

Library of Congress Cataloging in Publication Data

Broudy, Harry S
    Truth and credibility, the citizen's dilemma.

    (The John Dewey Society lecture series; no. 17; 1980)
    Includes index.
    1. Ethnics—Addresses, essays, lectures. 2. Truthfulness and
falsehood—Addresses, essays, lectures. 3. Education—Addresses,
essays, lectures.
I. Title. II. Series.
BJ1012.B73   111'.83'19   80-28305
ISBN 0-582-28208-X   AACR1

Manufactured in the United States of America

9 8 7 6 5 4 3 2 1

Acknowledgments

I would like to thank members of the John Dewey Society Lecture Commission—Gerald M. Reagan, D.B. Gowin and Mary Anne Raywid—for the opportunity to deliver the 1980 John Dewey Lecture. Professor Royall Brandis read the chapter on economics and gave me advice which, had I been able to follow it, would have improved its scholarly quality. To my colleague, Gordon A. Hoke, I am indebted for numerous bibliographical suggestions and lively discussion on the issues discussed in the book. I owe Dorothy, my wife, thanks not only for help in the preparation of the manuscript but for patience with my own efforts to do so.

Urbana, Illinois   H.S.B.
November 1980

Acknowledgment is also due to the following sources for their permission to reprint:

Excerpts from articles by Edward Cowan, Shlomo Maital, Linda Greenhouse, and Marvin E. Wolfgang. © 1980 by the New York Times Company. Reprinted by permission.

Excerpt from "Going . . . Going . . . Gone!" by Robert Hughes. Reprinted by permission from TIME The Weekly Newsmagazine; Copyright Time Inc. 1979.

Excerpt reprinted by permission of Sierra Club Books from *The Unsettling of America* by Wendell Berry, copyright © 1977 by Wendell Berry.

Contents

The purpose of political philosophy is precisely the creation of methods such that experimentation may go on less blindly, less at the mercy of accident, more intelligently, so that men may learn from their errors and profit by their successes.

John Dewey, *The Public and Its Problems*

Preface

Some religious rites include a prayer for purity of body and mind to make the ritual acceptable. In beginning a book on truth and credibility, a silent prayer for purity of heart and clarity of mind is in order. In such a venture one is exposed to the flanking charges of moralism and antiintellectualism. An editorial writer for the *Wall Street Journal* finds moralism in economics and politics "tiresome", and a syndicated pundit refers to a presidential blunder in foreign policy as "mere" moralism.

The distaste for moralism, one may suppose, is a form of the pragmatic reluctance to take the eye off the main chance; it may also reflect a distrust of claims to self-righteousness. Before questioning the righteousness of others, one should examine oneself for marks of smugness, sanctimoniousness, hypocrisy, envy, false modesty, and genuine immodesty. If only he who is without sins of this kind is qualified to cast the first stone, who dares claim to be so qualified?

Fortunately, words are not stones, and casting them to destroy the wicked is not the purpose of this book. It is addressed to those who have spent much of their careers urging the use of knowledge and reason in the affairs of a free and humane society. This book examines the relation between what Dewey called warranted assertion, our best approximation to truth, and credibility, or what might be called warranted commitment: the relation of a proposition to the person uttering it.

As to possible charges of antiintellectualism, I plead innocent to one form of it and possibly guilty to another. I do not reject the validity of science and its methods nor that such knowledge is a proud triumph of civilization. Mythical thought, extrasensory intuition and perception, and no amount of mutual grooming behaviour among the hermeneuticists of language and myth can compete with modern science as a description and explanation of physical phenomena. I can also understand the efforts to study human phenomena in the manner of physical science, that is to say, as if they were not human.

Problems with scientifically warranted assertions arise for the citizen only when they are put forward as grounds for decision in individual and public life. At that juncture, the citizen is confronted with two difficulties. One is how to decide between disagreeing experts; the other is restoring the relevance of highly abstract concepts to the human concrete reality from which they were initially abstracted. If worrying about this relevance gap is antiintellectual, then perhaps this book is guilty of the charge. In any event, I cannot repeat too often that the problem is not a scarcity of reliable knowledge but a superfluity of it.

My academic colleagues may be disturbed by the style of the discourse in this book unless it is kept in mind that it is written from the viewpoint of a U.S. citizen living in the last quarter of the twentieth century. He or she has been through the public schools and some years of postsecondary education. Whatever an average socioeconomic background might be, this citizen has it. Assuming that the citizen wishes to behave rationally and to take part in the political and social life of his country within the framework of democracy, he or she will try to use the best available information to debate issues and make decisions. The citizen's stance toward this information is not that of a scholar or specialist. Not all of the scholarly deficiency should be attributed to the citizen, however; much of it reflects my own limitations.

It may be appropriate to inform the reader that I am neither a Dewey scholar nor disciple. The invitation to deliver the John Dewey Society Lecture for 1980 reflects, I hope, my appreciation of John Dewey's contribution to an understanding of education and schooling. Dewey's doctrines are a touchstone against which all of us must test our arguments and a grindstone on which to sharpen them. In this country, at any rate, the Deweyan formulation of thought and action, teaching and learning, is one of the ineluctable intellectual "facts" of this century.

I ask the indulgence of numerous colleagues who have written on Dewey; from them I have learned much, although they are not cited explicitly. I also wish to apologize for sexist locutions such as "man," "humanity," "mankind," and the corresponding masculine pronouns. The syntax does not reflect my sentiments.

1

An Old Ghost Reappears

In what is perhaps one of the most radical proposals of the twentieth century, John Dewey argued with a straight face that a democratic society could also be a rational one, Plato's and other notables' views to the contrary notwithstanding. Dewey's thesis presupposed two unlikely conditions: (1) that a democratic society could be governed by a majority vote of enlightened citizens; and (2) that a system of schooling could produce this enlightened citizenry, generation after generation. Few, if any, historical precedents existed for either condition. No less radical was Dewey's prescription for enlightenment.

To be sure, Dewey did not invent the ideal of an enlightened state. The Enlightenment had captured the imagination of Europe in the eighteenth century, as well as that of the Founding Fathers in America. Benjamin Franklin and Thomas Jefferson, for example, were not ignorant of the discoveries of Isaac Newton, the rationalism of Descartes and Bayle, the writings of John Locke, and the French *philosophes*. They shared the Enlightenment's skepticism about the truths of religion and its faith in the powers of human reason to discover the universal principles that govern nature, man, and society.

Nevertheless, it was not at all obvious to the *philosophes* of France or the Founding Fathers that reason, although universal, was distributed uniformly throughout the population. Nor was it taken for granted that all individuals (albeit Jefferson regarded as a self-evident truth that they were created equal) could become equally rational. For Plato, only in the *aristoi*, an elite few, was reason the sovereign faculty keeping appetite and emotion under control. And even the elite could not be relied upon to the use reason for the good of the state without strenuous character training, divestiture of private families and fortunes, and a very special kind of education—philosophical. Even in its day these were outrageous as well as radical proposals.

Moreover, an enlightened society did not mean necessarily a democratic society. In Prussia, for example, an enlightened society was to be produced and maintained by an enlightened monarch. Thus Frederick II in 1781 noted that "...the sovereign represents the state; he and his people form a single body which can be happy only insofar as they are in accord. The prince is to society what the head is to the body; he must see, think, and act for the whole community in order to procure for it all the advantages to which it is entitled."[1]

Voltaire referred to the common people as *canaille* (dogs) "who need a god and a king to keep them in leash." Nevertheless, in this country and in most liberal societies, the republican and even the democratic forms of government were expected to prevail over the monarchical, an eventuality that would be probable and desirable if artificial constraints on enlightenment were removed. Education, freedom of thought, and the opportunity for collective deliberation about public problems were thought to be the necessary and sufficient conditions for actualizing the rational potential of humankind.

Education is what has been called an "enabling" right; that is, the public shall provide persons with resources that enable them to exercise their "permissive" rights. Thus if democracy implies the right to be informed about the public good, and if this implies a right to education, then the public has the duty to provide it.[2]

It is not surprising—indeed, it was almost inevitable—that numerous schemes for universal education to free the rational powers of man should be part of the Enlightenment. Rousseau (1712–78) provided a romantic version of this faith in education. Émile, freed from the conventions and superstitions of a corrupt society, would develop naturally into a rational human being reflecting what was naturally human. And there were many other schemes.[3]

This was to be expected. The school is one of society's means of controlling the consciousness of the public. Through formal instruction, it exerts a steady pressure on each generation intellectually and by informal methods morally. Consequently the school is the putative remedy of first resort for all social problems and predicaments. The schools would unleash a flood of intelligence wherewith to reform society, as science had done to flush away the superstitious, anthropomorphic thinking about the movements of the earth, the stars, and falling bodies, including military projectiles.

The American public school has operated on the Jeffersonian belief that an enlightened electorate in a free society would arrive at the best available solutions to public problems, especially if guided by a constitution and other quasi-sacred documents that defined and limited the powers of the state. The citizen could promote rational social action by voting for enlightened representatives who correctly construed the public good. There were differences of opinion, of course, as to what constituted the public good and the qualifications for enlightened representation of it. Some thought only men of special talent and spirit could do so; some felt that in a democracy one man could serve the public good about as well as almost any other.

To this enlightenment the school was to contribute, first, skills of communication and the rudiments of knowledge suitable for vocational use but also for the general cultivation of the mental powers. Second, the school was to introduce the pupil to the ideals of democracy, its official documents, its sentiments, values, and ethos.

In this view of education, schooling is no longer regarded as a privilege or a good to be provided by parents at their discretion. It becomes a prerequisite for exercising the rights and duties of citizenship, so the state has a *compelling* interest in seeing to it that future citizens are schooled. Latter-day libertarians, urging voucher systems, seem to have forgotten colonial experiments with private schooling and voluntary participation in publically supported schools. Just as not all the members of the congregation voluntarily learned to read in order to discover the true meaning of the Scriptures, so not all parents voluntarily sent their children to school in order to prepare for the duties of citizenship. The recent revival of efforts to break up the "monopoly" of the public schools in the name of freedom of choice, to be thoroughly consistent, should include the option of not going to school at all.[4]

The colonial schools and those that flourished in succeeding centuries worked on the assumption that standard subjects derived from the arts and sciences and organized to accommodate age differences would fulfill the political and cultural requirements of the new nation. It was a curriculum fashioned after that provided for the upper middle classes with some adjustments to working- and middle-class needs.

The humanistic aspects of the Enlightenment were represented by the study of suitable selections from literature and history. As late as the 1920s, pupils in the middle grades of the grammar school memorized portions of Daniel Webster's more famous orations and certain poems. They were taught as exercises in declamation, but it was no doubt expected that the very act of declaiming sentiments in elegant language would literally shape the minds, hearts, and language of the pupils. And who is to say that it did not?

The sciences, as is well known, did not enter the traditional classical curriculum readily; even when they were studied, it was as bodies of content—laws, accounts of experiments, problems, and where appropriate, mathematical formulas for solving them. One studied selected contents of physics, chemistry, and biology, especially if entrance into college was contemplated. Scientific method was something used by scientists. Pupils appropriated the results of their inquiries, and only in a few laboratory exercises did they sample the method itself. Modern science was an achievement of intellectual giants for which all humanity was supposed to be grateful and which educated men should try to understand.

DOMESTICATING SCIENTIFIC METHOD

The radical import of Dewey's doctrine consists in urging that the scientific method as used in modern science by scientists is no more and no less than the method of intelligence itself. In this view the hope of an enlightened democratic society rests not only on schooling but on schooling that embodies in its curriculum, organization, and modes of instruction the method of intelligence.

The method of intelligence is the hypothetico-deductive reasoning characteristic of scientific thinking. It is now familiar to us as the progression from problem to observation to formulation of hypotheses, to the testing of the hypotheses by instating the conditions that could be predicted from them. Dewey gave an informal version of it in *How We Think*, a justly famous little book that educators read and teachers took to heart.[5] The method has been called the Complete Act of Thought (CAT), and its importance for schooling lies in the claim that young and old, pupil and citizen, could use it to bring the scientific method to bear upon questions of both fact and value. Schools, by making pupils adept in the use of the CAT, could produce and sustain a rational democratic society. If Galileo and Newton secularized science, Dewey domesticated it, and therewith democratized it.[6]

Presumably scientific method frees us from the errors of superstition, custom, traditionalism, and, above all, from absolutisms—epistemic, religious, and political. Schools, public schools, teaching successive generations the method of intelligence, were to be the key to a rational democratic society. The American democratic public was not to be confused with the tumultuous *demos* of Athens or the Roman crowds demanding bread and circuses. On the contrary, its composition and procedures were modeled on a relatively small assembly of free citizens, uninhibited and unintimidated by noble lords of the manor or oligarchs of industry and business. This type of assembly was not uncommon in the small New England town or village. All the citizens could convene in a hall and transact the community's business face to face. They could debate the issues without electing representatives to do it for them.

The importance of this model for understanding the Deweyian faith in the CAT as a means of using the method of intelligence in collective deliberation cannot be overestimated. To make group use of the method of intelligence workable requires not only a willingness of men of good-will to reason together but the ability and resources to do so. No doubt there was a time when inhabitants of small enclaves could *make up their own minds* on the basis of their knowledge of the issues involved. It made sense for these citizens to believe that they had some control over their economic destiny if, as was likely, they were land-owning farmers, pro-prietors of small businesses, or independent craftsmen. Such a group could be expected to understand the problems of the community, estimate the consequences of optional solutions for themselves and for the group, and make what would qualify as a rational decision. Moreover, a group of this kind in a community of this kind could concentrate on finding means to achieve common goals because so much of the value system was held in common. Many of these values were attitudes quiescent or operating tacitly as unspoken premises that became explicit only when some policy or action threatened to contravene them. They included attitudes toward family, property, work, personal integrity, and civic duty. Today it is dif-ficult to find public assemblies that meet these conditions, and one of the results is that the public school finds it virtually impossible to instate the model in the classroom.

Some Dewey disciples sensed that in more heterogeneous groups deep value conflicts might stall the smooth flow of inference in the CAT. They proposed to deal with these psychological blocks by using group dynamics to determine what members of a group *really* wanted as distin-guished from what they thought or said they wanted. The CAT, plus group dynamics, was put forward as a method of arriving at a clarification of goals in group deliberation so that the method of intelligence would not be operating at cross purposes.[7]

Although Dewey was not altogether happy with the volume these disciples produced, he might have agreed that if a little group therapy were needed to sustain the method of intelligence, so be it, provided it was clearly understood that therapy was neither the method of intelli-gence nor a substitute for it. Perhaps Dewey's wariness of psychological therapy can be attributed to his belief that value conflicts were also amen-able to resolution, if the CAT is used to test "valuations." Granting that certain preferences were habitual valuations, following out their consequ-ences *in mente* would provide rational grounds for their "evaluation."

Dewey's method of intelligence is a far cry from the deductive rigor of classical rationalism, which in Descartes and Spinoza were exemplified by mathematical demonstration. Dewey had overcome his earlier ties with Emersonian Transcendentalism and Hegelian universalism. No Absolute Reason, natural or revealed, was needed. The rationalistic quest for certainty was futile and needless; a more modest and fruitful use of the powers of the human mind was available. What the natural scien-ces had done for beliefs about the workings of nature the CAT, taught to all and used by the ordinary citizen, would accomplish for understanding the conditions and nature of the good life in the good society. This was indeed a radical promise to the common man.

At the heart of the Deweyian theory of knowledge is the notion that truth is warranted assertion, and an assertion is warranted when, and only when, it is the conclusion reached by use of the CAT, the scientific method. The assertion does not have to be warranted by deduction from clear and distinct ideas, as Descartes had maintained. On the contrary, being warranted by the CAT meant that a hypothesis had been tested by confirming the consequences that followed from it. This testing, like the other steps of the CAT, could be carried on by anyone able and willing to undertake it.

RATIONALITY AND REASONS

Rationality can be a property of propositions or of persons. A proposition is rational if it follows logically from premises that imply it, or follows logically as an induction from instances; or if it is the conclusion of a hypothetico-deductive argument. All such propositions are warranted assertions, to be distinguished from assertions that are impulsive, capricious, or mystically inspired. In this sense, warranted assertions are contrasted with propositions for which the evidence is private and subjective. The rationality of propositions is not identical with their truth, for it may turn out that a statement for which one can provide no rational warrant does describe the situation to which it refers accurately; a prediction made on nonrational grounds may also turn out to be accurate.

When rationality is the property of a person, as in speaking of X as a rational person, it refers to the ability and general willingness to give or to entertain reasons. In this sense, rationality is a character trait. Do the reasons X gives or accepts have to be "good" reasons if he is to retain the attribute of rationality? In one sense, the answer is no, for X's attitude toward reasons may not be matched by cognitive ability to provide or recognize good ones. If X insists that there is a reason or cause for the eclipse of the sun or a long drought, he would be manifesting a rational attitude. But what if he advances or accepts the hypothesis that the eclipse or the drought is caused by the wrath of an angry god? Here is a combination of a rational attitude and a nonscientific reason. Religious fundamentalists may perform arcane and arduous intellectual feats of biblical scholarship to prove that World Wars I and II, the nuclear bomb, and travel to outer planets were predicted in certain scriptural passages. Are we to say that these scholars are not rational or that their arguments are not? Or that their arguments are correct on intellectual grounds, but that it is irrational to even consider them as rational?

Reasonableness or being reasonable is an informal and weak variant of rationality. A proposition is said to be reasonable if it "stands to reason" or if it does not go counter to common sense or common knowledge. The same qualifications apply to a reasonable person or attitude: it is reasonable if it is not contrary to common expectations and conforms to what most people would do or think under ordinary circumstances. So one can be reasonable even if one cannot give explicit reasons or even if the reasons are not warranted by strict logic or scientific canons of inquiry.

When we speak of the citizen acting rationally, we mean something more than being reasonable, although we take for granted that rational citizens will not, as a rule, be unreasonable in what they say and do. We do not expect them to be stupidly stubborn or stubbornly stupid, over-emotional, and the like, but when making decisions, especially on communal problems, we do expect them to rely on knowledge that is reliable, and warranted logically.

In practical life, of course, we do not rely on our own research to arrive at warranted assertions. In most areas on which we are called upon to pass judgment we cannot become do-it-yourself scholars, although every public library has a scattering of citizens trying to do so. Ralph Nader and Consumers Union encourage citizens to do their own research on social issues, or at least to utilize the research others have done. The latter option is the more realistic one even for college graduates who are "into" social activism on one front or another. For in the nature of the case, research and scholarship are highly specialized activities, and non-specialists have to take their procedures on faith.

Each discipline studied in school introduces us to modes of inquiry and canons of evidence in a field of knowledge. Sociologists tell us what constitutes good sociological inquiry; economists do the same for their field. The range of disciplines with which the citizen has to become familiar today is indicated in a list of questions suggested as suitable tests for the "educated" undergraduate. Among the twenty-four questions that such an undergraduate should be expected to answer were What is a black hole? Describe step by step the procedures by which water, gas, and electricity reach a modern home. Can cosmic rays, gamma rays, or X rays produce cancer? What is a corporation? Should electron guns and lasers be subject to regulation?[8] The methods of modern astronomy, physics, chemistry, and the other natural sciences are here taken as criteria for rationality in explaining eclipses, droughts, earthquakes, nuclear bombs. The wrath of an angry god as a cause of such phenomena is not inconceivable—in fact not a few do so conceive it—but it does not meet the requirements established by the consensus of the learned. Persistent refusal by X to accept these criteria would jeopardize his claim to rationality in certain quarters, and almost certainly in most educated ones.

RATIONAL ACTION—PRACTICAL REASONING

Rational action connotes something more than a rational attitude and a fund of warranted assertions. It requires practical reasoning, and this involves knowledge about goals, means, consequences—items that are not the field of any particular academic discipline. Such knowledge is not given in a package but has to be assembled in each practical situation by the agent from a mélange of relevant sources—experience with kindred situations, technical experts, circumstances that will affect the impact of the action on others, and many others.

Such general information might be gleaned from common knowledge; from newspapers, magazines, and other media; or from associates. Judgments of relevance, testing of options against consequences, and other evaluative maneuvers go on more or less informally in ordinary life. In this connection, it is easy to overlook and underestimate associates in the workplace, clubs, and barrooms as sources of information and influences on opinion. It is an open secret, for example, that college students make many of their scholastic decisions on the advice of roommates and drinking companions. In these informal associations, information ranges over rumors, gossip, inside jokes, spellbinder disquisitions, and a wide variety of special knowledge associated with diverse occupations. The plumber, carpenter, elevator operator, clerk, and farmer are sources of this kind. The barroom is an especially interesting source of informal "education." The conviviality of the place encourages challenges of opinions supported by bets. Batting averages of famous ball players, conundrums, puzzles, politics, and philosophy are topics of discussion, debate, and wagers. The betting is a challenge to credibility as well as manhood because it asks the speaker to prove the sincerity of his commitment by "putting his money where his mouth is," a primitive sort of existentialism.

Practical reasoning when employed by corporations or legislative bodies is called policy making or decision making and has attained the status of an academic speciality, often in a new department of the university. But whether the process is carried on by a consumer trying to judge the relative merits of peanut butter brands or a corporation deciding on the wisdom of a merger, practical reasoning is a nest of prudential syllogisms, each composed of a hypothesis about what is desired and sets of "if I do this, this will happen" and "I do or do not want this to happen." Informal and haphazard as much of the reasoning may be, it nevertheless makes sense to distinguish actions that have been "thought out" from those that have not been.

The citizen makes both personal and communal decisions. As an individual, one has to decide whether to purchase a residence in a certain neighborhood at a given price. But one may also be called upon to vote on a referendum to authorize a bond issue for the construction of a sewer system in that neighborhood. Both decisions are instances of practical reasoning; but the referendum decision demands a broader understanding of economic factors than does purchasing the house, and a wider consideration of pros and cons, benefits and debits, for the community as a whole. Yet the two kinds of decisions seem to be converging in their cognitive demands on the citizen. For the purchaser of an automobile or a house, an understanding of international trade and finance seems about as necessary as for assessing the merits of bond issues.

Thinking things out fell into disrepute during the reign of the counterculture. Feeling things out was regarded as a more human and interesting response to life. Going through the ploys of practical reasoning signified a lack of sensitivity to the liberated consciousness. Of course, there is a crassness about calculating whether or not to fall in love or relieve the sufferings of a fellow creature or risk pollution of the environment in return for a reliable nonfossil source of energy. Knowing when to be practical and when not to engage in prudential calculation is the mark of a finely tuned sensibility. Some poorly schooled people have it, and some highly schooled ones do not: all educated people should.

Nevertheless, the citizen making a decision affecting the public good cannot escape the duty to be rational because the consequences of such decisions may inflict the very pains and sufferings that the counterculture was so anxious to avoid or correct. The issue is not whether to be rational in these situations, but how rational even the educated citizen can be.

This question brings us back to the potentialities of the method of intelligence for a rational democratic society and to John Dewey's faith that in this direction salvation lies.

DEWEY'S SCHOOL AND SOCIETY

The influence of John Dewey on American education is not easy to assess. The application of his doctrine in the classroom is not an adequate measure of his influence on educational thinkers and writers; conversely, the literature turned out by these thinkers does not measure the indirect impact of the doctrine on school practice. The intellectual influence, it seems to me, far exceeded the pedagogical one. Like other acute insights into the nature of teaching and learning, the method of intelligence was doomed to degenerate into a series of routinized steps so that it could be applied with a minimum of intelligence. In a mass society, mass production of schooling is as inevitable as mass production of commodities. Mass schooling, like the manufacture of commodities, thrives on the division of operations into smaller and smaller tasks that can be performed by robots or robotlike workers. William H. Kilpatrick's translation of the CAT into the Project method of teaching paved the way for others to produce ready-made projects to be carried out in the classroom according to fixed procedures. Kilpatrick, no doubt, deplored this development, for it was the very antithesis of the "method of intelligence," but there seems to be an inexorable pedagogical entropy that destines all inspiration to end up in devices for rote memorization.[9]

Nevertheless, the CAT and the theory behind it remain as rebukes to

equating learning with rote memorization of prepackaged and preprocess-
ed results of other people's inquiry. It continues to serve as the conscience of educators. Not that rote memorization is dispensable in schooling or
bad as such. Some things have to be learned by rote for long-term reten-
tion and for recall on cue (e.g., the multiplication table). It would be a
silly waste of time to deduce the process from arithmatical axioms each
time a multiplication has to be performed. Yet it is no less silly to believe
that rule-governed behavior constitutes an education on any reasonable
construal of the term.

Dewey's influence went beyond pedagogy and school keeping. Because the CAT was a formula for social action as well as for the reconstruction of individual experience, its use by the schools to reconstruct
society was a natural consequence. Reconstructionism under the leadership of Theodore Brameld urged the school to become the vanguard of
social change in accordance with principles of Dewey's instrumentalist
theory of knowledge.[10] Understandably, conservatives construed this mission of the school to reconstruct society as a misguided doctrine at best
and a Red plot at worst. Whether the school should be a transmitter of
society's values rather than a shaper of them is still a live issue.

There is little doubt that the influence of Dewey's writings on the
ideology of school personnel was widespread. The rhetoric of liberal
democracy became part of the language patterns of professional education and was invoked even in schools innocent of liberal practices. It is
no accident that many of Dewey's followers were active in the Liberal
party in New York City and enthusiastic about the New Deal of the
1930s.

In the 1960s this brand of liberalism was branded as "tired" both by
conservatives who felt the country had more than enough of the New
Deal reforms and by counterculturists who believed that the doctrine was
impotent to effect the radical cultural change they thought necessary. Revisionist historians, moreover, questioned the "liberalism" of John Dewey himself with respect to many social issues: "Thus it seems to be the
case that Dewey more than any other American philosopher best articulated the concerns of the new professional middle class about the loss of
small town community; the fear of class conflict, violence, and revolution; the fear of the ignorant uncontrolled immigrant masses; the quest
for scientifically rationalized orderly change; the desire for a classless
meritocratic social order. . . ."[11] Recently, there seems to have been a
revival of interest in Dewey's writings, and it may portend a renewed
interest in his brand of liberalism.[12]

At this writing, the term "liberal" is no longer an honorific epithet
and certainly not an informative label. There are remnants of Franklin D
Roosevelt's New Deal liberals, but liberal intellectuals and politicians are
likely to be neo-conservatives and libertarians who deplore the efforts of
government in the field of social and economic services. Neo-Marxists

also distrust the *old* liberals. Radical chic and limousine liberals vie for publicity as friends of the poor and oppressed. But it is generally agreed that the real political agitation comes from special interest groups who vote their needs, wants, hobbies, or obsessions rather than party ideologies.[13]

Single-interest groups are not new in our political life. Each major industry subscribes to a version of the claim that what is good for General Motors is good for the country. Some of the great reforms (women's suffrage, the abolition of slavery and child labor) began as single-interest groups. In a highly interdependent society almost any enterprise of any size can claim to be a necessary condition for the viability of the whole social order. The prevention of pollution of rivers and lakes certainly has wide-reaching consequences; so has the maintenance of the purity of the atmosphere and half a hundred other good causes.

Dewey himself defined the good society as one in which the greatest variety and number of interests can be shared.[14] The CAT can help a group discover what and how much it can share, but it cannot of itself establish the validity of sharing or command a commitment to it. Sharability is one of those intrinsic values that embarrass a doctrine that denies the existence of intrinsic values.

The Dewey thesis holds, it seems to me, that the question What ought we as citizens do? can and should be answered by another query, namely, What can we know about the situation? What warranted assertions can we assemble as a justification for decision? It would follow that if the schools could enable the citizenry to answer the knowledge question, it would also help answer the "ought" question; the grounds for warranted belief are to be found in warranted assertions.

To some critics the tentative, experimental judiciousness of the method of intelligence, the willingness to weigh all sides, the unwillingness to make any principle ultimate is an unrealistic approach to social conflict and action. Warranted assertion and rationality in general assuage the philosophical passion for clarity of thought, but less cerebral passions suffuse the concrete situations in which public policy is debated and shaped.

Dewey's method of intelligence was liberalizing in the same sense that the Enlightenment was—it freed the mind and the polity from ways of thinking (if not always of feeling) that science had outmoded. These ways included not only what most educated persons would call superstitions but also ancient class distinctions and their corresponding codes of conduct. It encouraged examination of old assumptions and the formation of new hypotheses about human potentiality. Yet the citizen is about as likely to use the CAT in thinking through social problems as he is to assemble sophisticated weather reports in planning a picnic.

The weakness of the method of intelligence does not reflect a lack of knowledge or expertise or even the willingness of the citizen to employ it.

In small groups dealing with local situations not only the necessary knowledge but also knowledge about the motives of the participants are known or can easily become known. There is credibility as well as truth. In large social issues the network of motives, of oxen to be gored or fed by a particular policy, is so vast and intricate as to shake the confidence of the well-intentioned citizen. What can he believe?

In the closing decades of the twentieth century many thoughtful citizens are entertaining a possibility about as radical as that which Dewey envisioned. It is the suspicion, strengthened almost daily by events, that warranted assertion may not be sufficient grounds for warranted commitment. In other words, an enlightened citizenry willing to use information in making rational decisions may not be able to do so.

Can it be the fault of the educational establishment? If so, at what level? Surely not in the university research complex, for it is to this complex working with industry, the military, agriculture, and business that we owe so much of our technological advance. The sheer volume of knowledge utilized and exemplified by our economy, government, and communication almost exceeds our capacity to understand and appreciate.

Has, then, the lower school system failed? Many say so, but on a national scale this is hard to believe. The proportion of our population that has completed high school and college is at its highest level and compares favorably with other industrialized countries of comparable size and complexity. Our professions do not lack for personnel and our government for bureaucratic experts. That there are murky pockets of school ineptitude and perhaps failure does not darken the whole landscape so far as schooling is concerned.

As for democracy, we have had but one major civil war. The successions of political power have not been brought about by *coups d'état* and military juntas. We have managed our scandals peacefully. Civil rights and political liberties have not been abrogated, despite periodic exposés of FBI forays into privacy. The protection of civil rights has become a subspecialty for the legal profession. The press is free and does not hesitate to exercise that freedom. We conduct primaries and elections for months on end and at astronomical cost. The clamor for more participation by more groups and constituencies continues.

By all sensible criteria we can claim to have produced an enlightened citizenry and preserved a democratic form of society that with extraordinary vitality has survived wars and depressions. It is still the land to which thousands upon thousands of immigrants would like to come, and which its most articulate critics are loathe to leave. Why, when science, technology, and the means of communication are at their zenith, in a nation so long dedicated to democratic ideas and institutions, is there so much uneasiness about the present and skepticism about the future? Why cannot science, technology, computers, think tanks, and huge cadres of sophisticated administrators control inflation, solve the energy crisis, protect the environment, reduce crime, and eliminate poverty and racial inequality, political chicanery, class strife, and the clutch of other social evils that our mass media report and rehearse almost routinely?

One answer might be that the citizenry is still insufficiently enlightened. Would we do better if we knew more? The customary answer to the latter question has been yes, but the further question is more about what? Do we need more information or do we need to absorb more of the available information? Every cause pleads for more information to be provided for a public, preferably by the schools. Agencies are set up to gather and disseminate it. The government publishes so many helpful documents that it also has to publish a directory listing them. Every big industry has its public relations apparatus that works with the best communication facilities to make more information available. Libraries are stocked with hundreds of publications designed to inform, free of charge, anyone who wants to learn about almost anything. The labels on products carry lists of ingredients, processes, norms, and other data so plentiful that only the smallest print can be used. And yet the demand for more information continues unabated. Clearly we believe that if we or the public in general read more and listened more carefully, we would act differently with respect to our social problems.

We cannot act on information alone; the information must first be understood, then interpreted for relevance, and finally command belief and commitment. But what if the citizen cannot assess the truth of the available information or its import for action? Science has given us the criteria for warranted assertion about matters of fact, but where do we find the criteria for warranted acceptance of their import?

The citizen is confronted not only with knowledge that he cannot assess but he is also made aware that it is virtually impossible to carve out of the amorphous mass of interdependence a situation that can be bounded and defined for examination and judgment. And yet the method of intelligence would have us take all relevant consequences and connections into account.

While this book is not about Dewey's writings, it is concerned with their premise and promise, namely, that by meeting the logical demands of warranted assertion, an individual and a community can act rationally. If that claim is now less persuasive than before, is it because the identity between the grounds of warranted belief and the grounds of warranted commitment to act on those beliefs has been ruptured? And if so, what has ruptured it? The implications of such a rupture for the uses of knowledge in general and for education in particular are as perplexing as they are disturbing. Is it possible, or even thinkable, that after all our efforts to strip from the truth of propositions all the personal, moral, aesthetic factors, we may have to reintroduce them in some way? Do we have to dirty up the logic of inquiry with the conditions of credibility?

It will be objected that philosophers of science have abjured objectivity as an ideal of science. All observation, it is pointed out, is already compromised by hypotheses, hopes, desires, and fears. This is not the issue being discussed here because I am not challenging the truth claims of experts as such. Rather, it is that even when vitiating factors are corrected, warranted assertions may through de-moralization lose credibility.

CREDIBILITY AND EXISTENTIAL TRUTH

Credibility reintroduces the moral dimension to knowledge. For credibility has to do with motives, and motives are not true or false, but good or bad. A bad motive may lead to evil consequences, and a bad motive disguised as a good one may have the same effect. Thus motives, banished from epistemological and logical relevance by impersonal reason in the name of objectivity, return to raise the problem of the "truth" about motives. The truth about motives, however, takes us into a domain of reality inhabited by selves, largely created by selves, and construed by selves. It is the domain of what has been called *existential truth*, a kind of truth in which human selves are willing to live and which they verify by living in it.

Many dangers lurk in the vicinity of any discussion of the difference between truth and credibility. Orthodox philosophic doctrine holds that we cannot doubt what we *know* to be true, and we *know* when the logical conditions of inquiry have been met. To believe without adequate evidence or in spite of inadequate evidence are species of intellectual sin, and although now and then intellectuals commit the sin, they cannot in principle condone it. The quest for truth must be cleansed of all non-cognitive considerations. These considerations are sometimes acknowledged when the story of great scientific discovery is told, but they are not part of the content. They are items of gossip not held to be relevant to the validity of what is found.

From another camp an inquiry into truth and credibility alerts the faithful to possible blasphemy, which denies or might denigrate supernatural sources of knowledge. The heart, it is argued, has its reasons; and when the heart is guided by the truths of religion, one need not worry about truth or credibility.

Is, then, the question of truth and credibility another replay of the ancient conflict between faith and reason? Is an old ghost about to reappear? In a way, it is.

However, the conflict may be between different antagonists. Traditionally, faith was invoked to help the human mind accept the mysteries of religion. Certain doctrines of the Christian church, it was held, were not comprehensible to human understanding but were revealed to man. A leap of faith was necessary to accept the revealed truth, especially when, according to Tertullian, it was absurd. Later, it was argued by Thomas Aquinas that the doctrines of religion, whether revealed or not, could not be contrary to reason. In any event, faith is supposed to deal with a kind of reality that is sometimes called spiritual as distinguished from the physical kind.

There have been systems of thought e.g., materialism that denied the existence of nonphysical reality and dismissed it as a fantasy created by the imagination and transmitted by superstition. At the other end of the spectrum Idealism held that mind or mindlike reality was all that we could experience directly and indubitably. Attempts to study mind empirically, W.E. Hocking averred, only gave us knowledge about "near mind."[15] It is the role of this mindlike reality, the product of mind and its functions, that gives rise to the notion and relevance of credibility. For the same mind that acquires knowledge of objects can imagine those objects going out of existence; the same mind that produces truth is the source of error. It is difficult to decide which is the more important question: How can the mind achieve truth? or, How can the mind create error?

Human action, as we shall have repeated occasions to remind ourselves, moves between these two domains of reality, between the world of fact and that of value or the import of fact to the human reality. Credibility is what must be added to truth to validate that movement. Faith in our time is not a substitute for science or for the facts disclosed by science, nor is it needed to fill gaps in our knowledge left by science. On the contrary, the fiduciary dimension of thought is made necessary by the overabundance of factual information and sophisticated theory.

This book explores four general areas. The first are the obstacles to rational action in a modern, complex, technology-based society. Some of these are systemic; some originate in the individual reactions to what are believed to be generic threats to safety and sanity.

A second area discusses the obstacles to belief when information and theory from various sources and certified by various authorities fail to explain or remedy major social problems.

The third concern is with the de-moralization of knowledge in a society that promotes specialism in all walks of life, especially when that specialism is institutionalized in the university and the various professions.

Finally, there is the problem of re-moralization of rational inquiry and the roles of the educational establishment in it. Here will be raised the question as to the possibility of finding and elucidating a principle that can unify truth and credibility. Whether such a principle can be articulated and whether it can furnish the ground for some unified version of the public good in a fragmented society remains to be seen.

REFERENCES

1. Quoted in Henri Brunschwig, *Enlightenment and Romanticism in Eighteenth Century Prussia*, trans. Frank Jellinek (Chicago: University of Chicago Press, 1974), p. 17.

2. *See* Ralph Barton Perry, *Realms of Value* (Cambridge, Mass.: Harvard University Press, 1954), pp. 324 ff.

3. *See*, for example, chapters 12–15 in Frederick Eby and Charles F. Arrowood, *The Development of Modern Education* (New York: Prentice-Hall, 1940).

4. Inasmuch as formal schooling does not always gladden the hearts of pupils, it is an imposition from which such reluctant scholars may be freed by the courts and Civil Liberties Union in the name of human rights.

5. Boston: D.C. Heath, 1910, 1933.

6. The philosophical literature on the nature of scientific method and its relevance to education is vast. For a survey of this literature in relation to science education, see Robert H. Ennis, "Research in Philosophy of Science Bearing on Science Education," in *Current Research in Philosophy of Science*, ed. Peter D. Asquith and Henry E. Kyburg, Jr. (East Lansing, Mich.: Philosophy of Science Association, 1979), pp. 139–170.

7. R. Bruce Raup, George Axtelle, Kenneth Benne, and B. Othanel Smith, *The Improvement of Practical Intelligence* (New York: Harper, 1950). This could be regarded as a forerunner of values clarification as a method of moral education.

8. In a letter by Walston Chubb, *Harvard Magazine* 80 (July–August 1978): 7–8.

9. William H. Kilpatrick, *The Foundations of Method* (New York: Macmillan, 1925).

10. Theodore Brameld, *Patterns of Educational Philosophy* (Yonkers-on-Hudson, N.Y.: World Book, 1950), chap. 17.

11. Clarence J. Karier and David Hogan, "Schooling, Education and the Structure of Social Reality," *Educational Studies* 10(1979): 245–66.

12. For a good summation and discussion of the literature on the status of Dewey, *see* Joe R. Burnett, "Whatever Happened to John Dewey?" *Teachers College Record* 81 (Winter 1979): 192–210; also George R. Geiger's discussion in *The Philosophy of John Dewey*, The Library of Living Philosophers, vol. 2, Paul A. Schilpp, ed. (Evanston, Ill.: Northwestern University, 1939), pp. 337 ff. *See also* H. Gordon Hullfish and Philip G. Smith, *Reflective Thinking: The Method of Education* (New York: Dodd, Mead, 1961).

13. Perhaps the full flavor of the sort of liberalism that relied heavily on the resources of reason is caught in the recently published book by Ronald Street, *Walter Lippmann and the American Century* (Boston: Little, Brown, 1980). Lippmann was for 36 years the author of a widely syndicated column called "Today and Tomorrow" and also served as an editor of the *New Republic*.

14. *Democracy and Education* (New York: Macmillan, 1916), p. 97.

15. "Mind and Near-Mind," in *Proceedings of the Sixth International Congress of Philosophy*, ed. E.S. Brightman, pp. 203–15.

2

What and Whom to Believe

The conflict between faith and reason became central in the confrontation of the claims of religion and science or philosophy, especially if they supported incompatible accounts of the origin of the world, the nature of man, and the destiny of both. And although the incompatibility with philosophy characterized most, if not all, supernatural religions, it became acute with the advent of Christianity. Its doctrines of the Immaculate Conception, Christ as God incarnate, the Resurrection, and his role in Redemption all defied natural reason. These doctrines demanded faith in a revealed truth of a mystery to which philosophy, restricting itself to the powers of the human intellect, had to relate itself in some way.

One startling relation was proposed by Tertullian, who in the second century proclaimed the complete separation of faith and reason in matters of theology. *Credo quia absurdum* (I believe because it is absurd) expressed the radical chasm between the logic of the philosopher and faith in certain Christian doctrines. These were to be accepted on faith alone, and given the faith, there was no need to rationalize the revealed truth.

Saint Augustine, borrowing Anselm's phrase *Credo ut intelligam* (I believe in order to understand), gave the palm to theology, so that if intellect were to have access to any sort of knowledge, it would first have to be illuminated by God. When so illumined, the human intellect was a premonition of the state of blessedness in the afterlife in which all truth would be revealed.

The Arabian and Latin Scholastics, with the help of Aristotle, established the supremacy of philosophy over theology, but both were settled into parity by the interpretations of Saint Thomas Aquinas. Aquinas argued that all knowledge is of God, and all conscious beings know God in everything they know, for they are the effects of God. So God can be known from above by Revelation or from below by reasoning from effect to cause, and ultimately to the First Cause.

Attempts to *prove* the existence of God were successfully torpedoed by skeptics and rationalists, who demanded the kind of proof that in the nature of the case theists could not supply. The skeptic doubts the existence of a supernatural deity and challenges the believer to provide empirical evidence; the rationalist argues that none of the arguments adduced for the existence of God can sustain itself against counterarguments. For example, one version of the ontological argument for the *necessary* existence of God held that there is one concept, that of a perfect being, which must include the fact of existence as part of its perfection. Hence the existence of the concept establishes Divine being. The retort of Kant and others was that existence other than *conceptual* existence cannot be deduced from any concept whatsoever.

There were other arguments for the existence of God. Aquinas, for example, deduced the existence of God from the necessity of a prime mover, the First Cause, a being necessary to account for contingent being, a unique source of goodness in the world and of the order found in the world. However, none of these arguments has escaped unscathed.[1]

The issue is of more than theological or metaphysical interest; it becomes involved in every debate about the objectivity of moral standards. Homosexuals and advocates of liberal abortion laws find their most stubborn and powerful opposition among those who believe that God has marked these activities, among others liberated by the counterculture from moral disapproval, as contrary to human nature, which he created in his image. All forms of moral relativity must lock horns with the argument from religious faith in an objective code proclaimed directly or indirectly by a supernatural source.

It may be helpful before going further to indicate what is meant in this book by such terms as *reason, faith, knowledge, truth,* and *credibility*. By reason is meant the use of mind to acquire truth or knowledge to provide "reasons for our views, proofs for our conclusions, and grounds for our opinions."[2] This would include all forms of reasoning—inductive and deductive—and all forms of discursive, mediated knowing under *reason*.

Assertions for which reasons and proofs are unavailable or insufficient we accept or reject on other grounds: the credibility of their sources, compatibility with one's value system, congruence with beliefs about reality and their implications. Unless an assertion follows logically and necessarily from premises that are themselves "proved," we have to take something without proof, that is, on faith. Probability is a statistical measure of the faith needed to accept inductive generalizations. It takes relatively little faith to believe that the sun will rise every day from now until 2500, but much more that it will keep the earth's atmosphere unpolluted. That future samples of green apples, for example, will be sour in the same proportion as the samples examined so far also requires an act of faith.

We take much of what passes for knowledge on faith. We do not ourselves verify the findings reported by physicists, chemists, and biologists unless we happen to be one of them and working in a particular specialty. Only the specialist is familiar with the research, the literature, counterexamples, evaluations by "competent scholars." It would be unreasonable to expect the layman to know his way about in this maze.

FORMS OF FAITH

The citizen's difficulty in trying to assess the deliverances of experts is compounded when they disagree. On issue after issue a claim by experts that evidence shows that so-and-so is the case is immediately countered by the argument that the evidence is inconclusive or that the experimental design is faulty or that the sample is unrepresentative. Why, for example, should we believe the experts who condemn the use of tobacco rather than those employed by the tobacco growers and processors? Why should we take Linus Pauling's claims for vitamin C seriously and doubt the claims of Laetrile? Reliance on the credibility of authorities is now a necessity in those very realms that science has liberated from faith. Sometimes a superboard of prestigious authorities is appointed to decide between conflicting experts. Do we trust the findings of this board because it is more "expert" or because they have no vested interest in the decision?

The citizen who is concerned about the public good must suspend the disbelief engendered by the plethora of conflicting reports on facts and the cacophony of theories purporting to explain them. Unless the alternative views are all wrong, choosing none of them is itself a choice that can have important consequences. Not voting may not be an effective form of neutrality; not choosing between nuclear power and abolishing its use may be a fatal form of neutrality.

On some issues it is difficult to decide whether assertions are accepted on faith or on knowledge. Theists, for example, accept the existence of God on grounds that range from faith in a revealed "mystery," through reasoning that certain ideas of perfection could not have occurred to human minds had there not been a source of such perfection (the ontological argument), to claims that extrasensory perception and spiritual exercises of one kind or another put human beings in touch with a transcendent being. Still other theists hold that the very existence of ideals and reason in human minds is evidence of a power for rationality and good in the world.

An extreme form of knowledge through faith is found in the principle that ". . . it is likely that unlikely things should happen,"[3] from which Tertullian drew the conclusion that "Christ's incarnation was the most likely event of all: *Certum est quia impossible.*"

There is also William James' "precusive faith" expounded in *The Will to Believe* (1895), which holds that in some cases acting on the faith that something is possible may bring it into existence. As an example of the ontological creativity of the will, consider the doubts of the lover who fears rejection. If the declaration is made, there is the risk of rejection; if the declaration is not made, then the possibility of its acceptance may forever be destroyed. Choosing the bold alternative, if successful, literally creates a complex of experience that would not have existed without the act of will. There are of course, endless ploys to circumvent the need to make the choice. For example, one probes indirectly to find clues of possible success or failure. Or incidents are invented or created—dangers and crises—that will elicit response from the beloved without the danger of a direct declaration or adamant silence.

The intensity of faith varies over a wide range. Anguish over religious doubts touching on the very possibility of salvation is a highly intense experience. Deciding on whether to invest in bonds or stocks is perplexing but hardly intense enough to cause anguish. The uncertainty attending decisions on the conduct of life increases as the potentialities for good and evil are randomized.

Can we believe A when he asserts P? What is implied by this question?

1. It could mean, in the simplest sense, to ask whether A is a liar. If A has a reputation for lying, there may be reason to believe that he is doing so now. But notorious, habitual, indiscriminate liars are a minor problem for the citizen, although they can be a nuisance when they participate in debates on public issues. The liar who twists the truth to serve some interest is the troublesome case. Whether A is lying in a particular instance has to be determined by examining his motives as well as the consistency of his statements in explicating or defending P.

2. It could mean Has A the knowledge and skill to legitimate his assertion of P? Does he have the proper guild credentials to permit the inference that he is in a position to know? This is the expertise or reputational criterion of credibility. A could be mistaken about the truth of P if it required expertise that he did not have or could not have acquired. Passionate advocates of causes are likely to make statements that are not based on reliable evidence. Many assertions regarding the merits and faults of schools and teachers fall into this category. So do many pronouncements on environmental pollution, the dangers/benefits of nuclear

energy. It is simply the case that on many important issues many persons with access to the press do not *know* what they are talking about.

In these circumstances the credentialling system provided by the various academic and professional guilds provides the citizen with some help. The press, fortunately, is generous with the labels of reputational credibility. The "renowned" institute, the professor at a "distinguished" university, the officers of a "prestigious" society are familiar examples. Speaking as loudly as such assurances of credibility is material success. The lawyer who commands fees in six figures is presumed to be more expert than those who take much more humble fees. In the professions the tendency to measure expertise and credibility by money rewards is growing. The heavy dependence on reputational credibility, however, puts the reputational criteria themselves into question. How credible are the certifying agencies? Can their judgments be trusted?

3. Does A have a motive that would be favored by the acceptance of P? For example, the tobacco institute argues that the evidence for the health hazards of smoking is faulty by scientific criteria. But the opponents of smoking discount such arguments not only on what they consider to be scientific grounds but chiefly on the motives of the tobacco interests. A citizen trying to make a decision on policy regarding the use and control of tobacco can take one or the other interpretation of the evidence either on scientific or credibility grounds. On most social issues, he may have to make the choice on grounds of credibility.

It would be a mistake, however, to think of our hypothetical citizen whose epistemological predicaments constitute the theme of this book as morally pure in intention and unbiased in judgment. He is not an impartial observer, and this complicates further his attempts to assess the truth of P and the credibility of A who assets P. He too has interests that are served better by one set of propositions than by another. He construes situations as relevant to his own interests and when he goes beyond them, it is to the interests of others and how they facilitate or inhibit each other. The citizen's frustration with knowledge comes from his inability to discern clear directions for serving these interests.

Nevertheless, in a democratic society the citizen is expected to consider the public good—especially when individual advantages or disadvantages are not clear and overriding. The electorate, on any given issue, can usually be divided into (*a*) those who vigorously espouse it, (*b*) those who strongly oppose it, and (*c*) those who are impartial as to the outcome and can be persuaded to support one of the first two groups. This uncommitted middle group is the proper target for political debate and the one that can be expected to make the decision in the name of the common good.

Only when the citizen is in this middle group does he become the paradigm of the enlightened member of the democratic polity trying to act rationally in behalf of the common good. As the ramifications of public issues become more widespread and more pervasive, there are fewer and fewer issues on which one can take the middle ground. If, for example, the political situation in a distant country does not affect my pocketbook or that of my family or my firm, then I can read about it or listen to a Public Broadcasting System panel as a more or less impartial observer ready to be persuaded by the facts of the situation. If, however, that nation is so related to other nations that it can play a strategic role in a possible war about the supply and price of petroleum, then I may no longer be in the middle group waiting to think and act judiciously. I may be at one of the extremes with overriding concern in the outcome. Where one's interests lie and where one can be an impartial observer are themselves primary questions for the well-intentioned citizen. Unfortunately, these questions have to be answered by the very same sources of information and the citizen's assessment of them, and the same considerations force him to shift from "What can I believe?" to "Whom can I believe?"

GROUNDS FOR BELIEF—SCHOOLS

An obvious first answer would be that you can believe what you learn in school. The reliability of the school as a source of knowledge is the premise for the conclusion that accessibility to schooling by all children is a necessary condition for an enlightened citizenry. Nothing, therefore, is more dismaying than a challenge to the adequacy of the knowledge it purveys. That challenge can be to the truth of what it teaches or to its credibility. If the school is committed to teaching warranted assertion as defined by the scientific community, then it expects the community to accept the school's judgment on what is to be taught. Not even the hard sciences are wholly immune to the objection that what is being taught ought not to be believed.

What, for example, is the truth about evolution? Does biology have it? Or have the Creationists a right to have their version of what "really" happened taught in the schools? Once the school moves into the social sciences, invoking the intellectual authority of economics, sociology, anthropology, or political science is a futile ploy. The furor over *Man, A Course of Study* in the 1970s is an example of what a community can do with materials that purport to be warranted assertions. The objectors accused the authors of subverting the curriculum in favor of liberal ideologies, although the course claimed to be based on assertions warranted by social scientists. The course and its dissemination received substantial financial help from the National Science Foundation (a prestigious scientific organization). But the protests mounted; one protest characterized it as a "pernicious attempt to spread the religion of secular humanism." Undoubtedly, the course did offend the mores of many people in many communities that do not look to the sciences for guidance in such matters as war and sexual practices. By 1975 the MACOS, controversy reached Congress when it was charged by Representative Conlan (Republican from Arizona) that the MACOS materials were "full of references to adultery, cannibalism, killing female babies and old people, trial marriage, and wife swapping."[4]

Especially awkward for the public schools are the accounts of the civic and political process. Political action in all societies, but certainly in a democratic one, is suffused by a self-serving rhetoric. This is only to be expected because the rhetoric is intended to persuade the body politic to feel and vote in one way rather than another. Sophisticated adults understand this and discount a good deal of it, but young children may not. The school operates on the principle that it must reinforce the ideals the community professes and not the behavior that it tolerates. Yet it is difficult to keep up the pretense that the behavior of officials, elected and appointed, does not violate professed ideals. For one thing, the mass media are exposing the pretense daily; almost hourly. The peccadillos of politicians become media events. How much of this can the school teach as part of the social studies or social science curriculum? How does a junior high school social studies class handle Watergate?

Even at the high school level it is difficult to imagine a teacher characterizing the democratic process as "an unending game" in which rivals for public office charge each other with hypocrisy, and that "as each side tries to destroy the credibility of its rivals, politics becomes a treadmill of dissimulation and unmasking."[5] Can the school curriculum do anything with this game? Indeed, who can qualify as a disinterested analyst of the game? Are the intellectuals of the academy so qualified? Not likely, if, as Shklar says, "For the observer of ideologies it is clear that the basic hypocrisy affecting all of them is the pretense that the ideological needs of the few correspond to the moral interests of the many. It is a hypocrisy to which all politically active intellectuals, who generally are also extreme anti-hypocrites, are especially given."[6]

As will be noted in a subsequent chapter, the academic guilds have high credibility within their own field of expertise, but even there one finds cliques, fashions, and pecking orders. Scholarship, too, is an endless game of unmasking the errors of existing theories and the creation of new ones, and is not immune to self-interest.[7]

Thus, the revisionist historians, including those writing on education, not only challenge the "facts" about colonial schools or slavery or working conditions found in the conventional history books, but they also advance learned defenses of the hypothesis that the bourgeois ideologies guided their selection of the "facts." In other words, they are advising the reader not only to read the text for what it says but also to ask who said it and why.[8]

In the same vein are the books arguing that the school curriculum is not objective truth, description, and analysis, but reflects the interest of social power groups. Classical education in France, according to Émile Durkheim, served the interests of the Catholic church.[9] Raymond Williams and Pierre Bourdieu have made similar arguments about the curriculum and class interests.[10]

Unfortunately, these exposes are themselves not immune from the credibility question. Who says this and why are queries relevant to all ideologues and ideologies, but there is a difference between debunking as an academic occupation and the assessment of certified information and knowledge by the citizenry as a rationale for choice and action. This may become clearer when some of the circumstances that frustrate the desire of the intelligent citizen to act rationally are examined.

The moment enlightened self-interest is admitted as a legitimate motive for action, the knowledge put forward as a justification for action is liable to the taint of self-interest. If previous times have been dubbed the age of skepticism with regard to religious truth, then ours may be the age of skepticism with respect to the impartiality of all information, when invoked as a rationale for action. It is no accident that in an age of triumphant science and technology, cultism, fantasy, and science fiction should also flourish.

BRAND NAMES AND BRAND PERSONS

It is not accidental that in an age of mass production of goods and services, brand names should acquire importance. At first, the brand name was a pledge of quality guaranteed by the character (reputation) of the company, and for this pledge the customer paid a premium over nonbrand products. Consumer advocates who are earnest advocates of more "information" so that shoppers can make intelligent choices have succeeded in crowding lots of information on labels. Comparing the labels should enable the customer to dispense with the extra cost of brand-name assurances of quality.

Of course nothing of the kind happens. Reading labels does not help the customer judge quality. More useful information is given by *Consumers Union*, which publishes ratings of products, saying boldly and clearly that this brand is better than that one, and not to mind the advertising or the labels. But why does one trust—if one does—*Consumers Union*? The main reason is that it does not accept advertising in its pages; a secondary reason is that it purports to base its ratings on research. However, research would not have the same fiduciary force, if the publication did take advertising from the firms selling the rated products. The brand-name phenomenon is a pedestrian but significant witness to the difference between truth and credibility. We do not trust the brand because we *know* that it tells the truth about the product; we believe what is said about the product because we trust brands. What really goes into the product remains a mystery to the consumer, despite all the information.

Claims for credibility have to be stated in the language of authenticity, sincerity, purity of heart, as well as in the language of warranted assertion. These claims have both moral and intellectual dimensions, the former having to do with the motivation and sense of responsibility of the advocate; the latter with the objective conditions of inquiry. This duality is disturbing because the search for truth has systematically tried to free itself from moral and personal considerations. The credibility problem legitimates such questions as *cui bono*? Who stands to profit? Who stands to lose? as epistemologically relevant.

In a way, this is reminiscent of trial by ordeal. For example, putting a hand in the fire without harm was regarded as proof of truth-telling. However, the connection between trial and truth required a supernatural intervention to make it plausible. The willingness or unwillingness to undergo a lie-detector test is a distant cousin to the ordeal as a test of credibility. Here the supernatural connection is downgraded to a neurological one. Blood pressure and glandular responses are taken to be above suspicion, not because they are above (or below) lying, but rather because they have not, as yet, been taught how. Some day, with appropriate biofeedback techniques, we shall outwit the integrity of our glands, and they will outwit the polygraph.

The locutions "He has an honest face," "That's a dignified building," and "I've got a piece of the rock" are examples of visual images of character traits. Such images, of course, are the stock in trade of the arts. They are the expressive apparatus of art. For if art does anything distinctive, it is to provide images of feeling, images that convey human import. Many of our credibility judgments depend on such images. Social enclaves, one may suppose, standardize sensory images of honesty, sincerity, duplicity, and other character traits. These serve as immediately comprehended signals for social intercourse. Such stereotypes are the vehicles of mass communication. As might be expected, these character trait images are exploited by the mass media to achieve credibility for persons, ideas, and products. The Prudential Insurance Company, for example, has been very successful in exploiting Gibraltar for this purpose.

The credibility of events also depends on aesthetic properties. An outstanding example is the continued skepticism with which the empirical accounts of the John Kennedy assassination are regarded. Not a year passes without someone claiming that evidence has been found to show that it "couldn't have happened" the way the Warren Commission said it did. One might ask why this persistent search for another account, and one answer is that to be credible the story would have to be dramatically adequate; the cause should be as significant as the effect. A conspiracy theory would be far more dramatically effective than what the Warren Commission decided was the true story. The artist rather than the scientist will determine what "really" happened.

These observations on credibility and truth seem prosaic when compared to the debates about faith and reason in philosophy and theology. Nevertheless, they are important to the citizen who is seeking clues to credibility. He is tempted to look about for what might be called "brand name persons" whom one can believe no matter what they say. Perhaps the citizen needs them to counter the bewilderment by experts to avoid playing out the drama of life in the theater of the absurd.

There is no lack of candidates for the role of brand-name credibility figures. Cult leaders, charismatic evangelists in and out of the pulpit, and astrologers are no strangers to the scene. And although they attract followers who do crazy things and believe even crazier theories, they also create nonbelievers and deriders. So while these groups multiply, there is little danger of any one of them capturing a majority or even a great minority of the population at large, let alone of intelligent and well-intentioned citizens.

Among the "brand name" credibility figures on whom the citizenry depends heavily are academics, professionals, and journalists. Each of these groups is proud of its objectivity, allegiance to the truth, and to the welfare of the society as a whole. They reaffirm these loyalties at every opportunity. In subsequent chapters there will be occasion to examine these protestations.

With journalists the question of credibility is especially relevant. For one thing, they speak and write on matters that are not within their field of specialized knowledge. They report what the generals say about war, what the State Department says about international affairs, what economic experts say about inflation, recession, and the like. By comparing what specialists say, they often smoke out inconsistencies, hidden facts, and motives. They are watchdogs of credibility, but rarely of their own. Some journalists earn the confidence of the public for reasons that are not always obvious. Perhaps they have the aesthetic properties that inspire it: they look as if they would not tell lies or twist the truth to their own advantage.

Nevertheless, it would be difficult to name an occupational group that is more closely related to the interests of our hypothetical citizen. They are more likely than technical experts and professional specialists to see problems in their existential concreteness and complexity; they can put themselves in the place of the citizen who does want to make sense out of his own life and of the social order in which he has to live it. A free, competent, and morally sound press is the citizen's best ally.

The class of journalists should be broadened to include other opinion makers and interpreters of the social scene. Editors, critics, clergymen, and a wide array of intellectuals also have access to the public ear and make their living by addressing and advising this public. It is through their utterances and writings that the intelligent citizen arrives at conclusions about social issues rather than through his own investigation of the facts or the reports of technical experts.

One would think that among the conglomerate that constitutes the opinion makers would be included philosophers, a tribe traditionally associated with the love of and search for wisdom. But one searches in vain for wisdom as a department of instruction in our colleges and universities, and if a naive student were of a mind to find out where on the campus he or she could study wisdom, the chances that the philosophy department would be recommended would be small; and the more "prestigious" such a department is, the smaller the chance would be. Formal philosophy in the last two or three decades has devoted its expertise pretty largely to the logical and linguistic properties of discourse, especially philosophical discourse. This moved one of my colleagues to note that God, freedom, and immortality were discussed in the courses in literature, whereas the properties of language were studied in the department of philosophy. In recent years interest in social philosophy and substantive ethics has revived perhaps as a response to the social activism of students in the late 1960s and early '70s, but perhaps even more because virtually every profession is expanding its practice into areas that raise ethical problems. But "professional" philosophers are still at some distance from the opinion makers, let alone the movers of events.[11]

REFERENCES

1. For a discussion of these four relationships, *see* Knut Trangy, "Thomas Aquinas," in *A Critical History of Western Philosophy*, ed. D.J. O'Connor (London: Free Press of Glencoe, 1964), chap. 6.

2. G.J. Warnock, in *The Encyclopedia of Philosophy*, ed. Paul Edwards (New York: Macmillan, 1967, reprint ed., 1972), 7: 84.

3. Aristotle *Rhetoric*, bk. 2, chap. 23.

4. U.S. House of Representatives, *Congressional Record*, House (9 April 1975). H. 2585. For a full discussion, see Jon Schaffarzick and Gary Sykes, eds., *Value Conflicts and Curriculum Issues* (Berkeley, Calif.: McCutchan, 1979), pp. 8 ff.

5. Judith Shklar, "Let Us Not Be Hypocritical," *Daedalus* 108 (Summer 1979): 12–13.

6. Ibid., p. 12.

7. An example of academic involutions and convolutions is a recent book that traces the theories of Freud, Marx, and Lévi-Strauss to the Jewish intellectuals' "ordeal of civility." What purport to be scientific theories of society, Cuddihy argues, are by the very tenets of these theories ideologies resulting from psychosocial circumstances. John Murray Cuddihy, *The Ordeal of Civility* (New York: Basic Books, 1974).

8. For example, Samuel Bowles and Herbert Gintis, *Schooling in Capitalist America: Educational Reform and the Contradictions of Economic Life* (New York: Basic Books, 1976). Also Michael W. Apple, *Ideology and Curriculum* (London: Routledge & Kegan Paul, 1979).

9. *The Evolution of Educational Thought: Lectures on the Formation and Developments of Secondary Education in France*, trans. Peter Collins (Boston: Routledge & Kegan Paul, 1977).

10. Raymond Williams, *The Long Revolution* (New York: Columbia University Press, 1961); and Pierre Bourdieu and Jean-Claude Passeron, *Reproduction in Education, Society, and Culture* (Beverly Hills, Calif.: Sage, 1977). *See also* Jean Anyon, "Ideology and United States History Textbooks," *Harvard Educational Review* 49, no. 3 (1979), for further references on this topic.

11. Among the notable exceptions is Sidney Hook, whose interest in social issues is summarized in his recent collection of essays, *Philosophy and Public Policy* (Carbondale, Ill.: Southern Illinois University Press, 1980).

3

Obstacles to Rational Action

Why, in the closing decades of the twentieth century, when every discipline is cultivated by scholars and experts unmatched in number and quality, when communications are approaching instantaneity, and when the proportion of our educated citizens is greater than could have been imagined a half century ago, are we so troubled about our ability to control our lives?

It would seem that now, if ever, rational control of our lives should be within reach. If the inhibiting factors are not the lack of knowledge or technology to apply that knowledge, then some other inhibitors are frustrating us. A few possible candidates for this role are the collapse of custom, technological overload, informational overload, the pitfalls of planning, and the randomization of good and evil.

COLLAPSE OF CUSTOM

On the face of it, to act at the behest of custom is the antithesis of rational action, although it would be reasonable to suppose that what had been done in a certain way for a long time probably had some inherent survival value. Rational action means to act after careful consideration of goals, alternative means, and possible consequences. Nevertheless, there is a real and important sense in which a society where all action was rational in this sense might be less efficient than one in which some portion of conduct was left to the direction of mindless custom.

Custom is the flywheel of the social engine. It sustains a smooth flow of power despite the occasional sputterings of the several pistons. In a stable society many decisions are made more or less automatically in conformity with well-established rules. Each institution—the family, industry, the church, the school, the government—has its own momentum (some would call it inertia) of custom so that for a wide range of action little deliberation is required. As this momentum is slackened, the need for conscious decision increases.

For example, several decades ago, a person in tattered garments, with unkempt hair and untidy beard, would have been perceived immediately as a doubtful character; a tramp, perhaps, of whom one should steer clear on a dark and lonely street. Today, visual clues provided by clothing, general appearance, and demeanor give no reliable basis for distinguishing male from female, tramp from professor, a prostitute from an heiress seeking a "meaningful relationship," a happy hippie from a mean mugger. A malelike figure approaching unsteadily may be under the influence of alcohol or heroin; he may want to talk politics, take your wallet or your life, or both.

Or to take another example, it was customary when meeting a friend whom one had not seen or communicated with for some time to inquire after members of the family. It was assumed that the friend had many informative things to say about spouse and children: items boring to all but good friends. Today such routine inquiries are ill advised. Rather than being regarded as a lack of interest, not to inquire may very well be taken as a welcome escape from having to tell about the divorce, the elder son's running away and doing heaven knows what and where; the daughter's experiments with sexual liberation, and a dozen other embarrassing developments. It is prudent to wait until the friend volunteers information about the family. This marks a great change in custom; one has to take thought about what previously was a matter of routine social behavior.

What does one wear to a dinner given by the dean of the college? What gifts does one bring when courting (dating)? Who pays for the dinner check when the woman earns three times as much as the man? What does one say to a dinner partner if fear of being accused of male chauvinism precludes making conventionally gallant compliments? Or what does one do if the dinner partner construes such compliments as sexual advances? These and scores of other behaviors are examples of *quod est cogitandum* instead of custom-governed actions, falling under the general rubric of manners. Manners have been regarded as minor morals because not to "mind one's manners" is to interfere with the flow of behavior along the grooves of custom, and is to be regarded as a willful or ignorant disregard of what is already established as "right."

The greater the number and diversity of unreliable signals, the more we have to pay attention and give thought to each situation. We cannot reserve inquiry, deliberation, and judgment for important decisions—all are *prima facie* important and demand explicit attention. As a result, the anxiety level rises over an ever broadening area of experience.

Nature furnishes a physiological analogue. Breathing, circulation of the blood, digestion, hormonal balance, beating of the heart, and many other vital functions are not left to conscious choice and control. One becomes conscious of these functions only when their routine is disturbed. On a cultural level, proscriptions of incest, cannibalism, patricide, and murder in many societies are beyond the pale of reflection. They are what William Graham Sumner called *mores*, norms of conduct grown out of folkways that somehow had come to be connected with the public welfare. To disobey them was to risk disaster for the group, and the codification of such mores became the basis of law. To question the rightness of such mores, Sumner noted, was unthinkable because they defined what was right.[1] Even in modern societies, to question the rightness of taboos against incest or infanticide is regarded as an intellectual affectation or as a symptom of psychopathology.

When such mores cease to be taken for granted, a social rebellion may be in the offing. Some of these rebellions are truly revolutionary; the recent changes in the sexual mores and marriage, for example. Others, although they annoy the senior generation, after a while are accepted as relatively harmless changes in fashion; for example, some of the changes in clothing and hair styles. It is not always possible to distinguish changes in the mores from changes in fashion.

When every transaction with a lawyer, physician, plumber, and business establishment has to be formalized by contracts and checked in every detail, energy is drained from substance to procedures. As will be noted shortly, some of this increased need for deliberate thought and choice is occasioned by technological and informational overload. Some of it results from the fact that automated control of complexity is itself complex, witness the system of thermostatic controls in a modern office building.

The collapse of custom is to be expected of an age in which some of the most active minds are engaged in revealing its irrational and nonrational components. One of the most familiar scholarly activities is to demonstrate that a given custom was at one time reasonable (albeit by modern standards perhaps not rational), but that it persisted long after the reasons for it disappeared. Of course, it will not escape the notice of the social observer that as one set of customs is abandoned, another set takes its place. Scholarship itself has its customs. Attempts to render all action orderly, systematic, and conscious complicate life and sharpen the need to be wary in all things. Rather than increase confidence in the ability to control our lives, they serve to underline our inability to do so.

TECHNOLOGICAL OVERLOAD

Technology, having progressed so brilliantly and rapidly, should greatly enhance the potentialities for rational action. It is our century's answer, moreover, to complexity and drudgery. Unfortunately, it does not always work out that way.

Rational action is hampered by the leapfrogging character of technological progress. The principle is fairly simple. A technology for increasing the efficiency of a function—for example, computers—is discovered. To make the technology profitable, its use has to be large enough to warrant a large capital investment. New uses for the computer have to be discovered or invented. Bright inventive people do so, and advertising and promotion are activated to create a mass market. If the promotion succeeds, the technology is overloaded. It now cannot handle the enlarged demand with the ease and speed that made it so efficient in the first place. To be sure, more is accomplished in less time, but more is left unaccomplished at the same time, so that there is a net increment of frustration. This frustration is expressed by blaming and deriding the computer. Blaming the computer is a stock item of everyday humor. It is the marvel and scapegoat of our time. When magic is promised, miracles are expected. Computerizing the post office, airline reservations, banking and business transactions are familiar examples of technological overload. Although the volume of transactions has been increased dramatically, the overload creates delays and mistakes that require complicated remedial procedures.*

There is no lack of horrible and horribly funny examples of computer overload. Some of these result from a reduction of checking, an overreliance on the infallibility of the machine. Not long ago it was reported that 1500 or so rodents used in a research project on the relation of cancer to gerontology died because a computer supposed to control temperature failed and the temperature rose too high. But why not check the reliability of the computer periodically, perhaps frequently? Because the "savings" that warranted heavy investment in the machinery would be dissipated. Furthermore, why check the more perfect machine by a less perfect one?

If one is to act rationally on the basis of information furnished by machines, then how large are the stakes that we can wager on the reliabil-

---

*One tiny mistake by a postal employee in recording a change of address resulted in three months of effort to correct the series of errors perpetrated by a complicated computer system of a national credit card company. Depositing a check to open a bank account in California, I was told that it would take ten days for it to clear the Illinois bank on which it was drawn, longer than it takes to make the round trip in an automobile.

ity of the machine? These seem like trivial questions fit for jokes, but more, and more important, issues and decisions depend on these machines. To have to check each time for "computer error" adds to the burden of watchfulness that ordinary life imposes. Is it efficient, for example, to check every item in a bank statement every month, the tax return made out by an accounting firm, scores of statements and invoices that constitute the fabric of ordinary household finance for computer error?

Computer breakdowns have been blamed for dangerous traffic snarls over airports, the monitoring of controls in nuclear power plants, not to speak of many procedures in hospitals and research laboratories that have been put under the electronic care of machines. How can these machines achieve the credibility that would make their benefits less stressful for those who are supposed to benefit from them?

The answer, it would seem, is to combine them with the moral concern of a human agent who assumes responsibility for their proper functioning. Such agents are needed, despite the number of redundant backup machines designed to monitor machines, for machines are not "concerned."

An example of this combination of technological ingenuity and absurdity is furnished by BART, the Bay Area Rapid Transit System, which was highly publicized as being virtually entirely automated. Tickets are sold by machine and machines figure out the fares. The trains move from station to station, starting and stopping at the signals from machines. More recently, however, according to a report in the *Wall Street Journal* by Victor F. Zonana (9 September 1980), the transit authority spent $1.3 million to permit manual car signaling, or running the train by hand. As it happens, the automatic 80-mile-an-hour system fails about 20 times a week. And when this happens, the train must crawl back to the yard while behind it cars pile up for miles.

A monumental 30-mile traffic jam was caused in New York City by a single faulty relief valve on a propane truck; the leak was finally stopped by two policemen using a $4 plumber's plug. The New York City blackout of 1977, it has been argued, might have been contained, had not the circuit breakers failed to close at key moments. Two false alarms by the Pentagon's early warning systems when they reported a Soviet nuclear missile launch were caused by a dime-sized computer circuit worth 46 cents.

These anomalies are amusing, but they undercut our reliance on technology to render action more rational and efficient. The inability to keep the use of a technology down to an optimum load is a consequence of the economics of large-scale production, which, in turn, is dictated by economic incentives. The demoralizing effect of such incentives infects the potential of technology for rational action. It is also an example of our inability to predict and control the interconnecting strands of influence energized by any important technological innovation.

The dialectic of technology overload also applies to personal conduct. For example, fifty years ago a coast-to-coast trip took several days or a week. Today it is possible to leave one coast at 7 A.M., deliver a lecture or attend a business meeting on the other coast, and be home by midnight. This remarkable acceleration, instead of giving us more leisure, increases the number of such trips scheduled. The improved technology is not used to improve the quality of life, but rather to increase the density of events with which one has to cope. Life is not made easier by the technology, but busier, often in spite of the individual's better judgment.

INFORMATION OVERLOAD

The rational U.S. citizen, one must suppose, would wish to take care of his health. To this end he reads with care the pronouncements of medical authorities, governmental bureaus, and consumer protection agencies on such matters as diet, exercise, smoking, carcinogens of all sorts and environmental pollution.

Despite the flood of information, other information tells us that the American public is not acting rationally. Report after report deplores the eating habits of the population; carelessness about immunization, smoking, and the use of drugs; and gross disregard of life and limb on the highways. Some of this disregard of information must be charged to lack of self-discipline. A Senate Select Committee on Nutrition and Human Needs suggested that we ingest 30 percent fewer calories from fats, 45 percent fewer calories in refined and processed sugars, 70 percent more in complex carbohydrates and naturally occurring sugars, and cut our cholesterol intake in half and our salt intake two-thirds. But most tasty foods are rich in these ingredients. Enjoyable habits are just too hard to give up, especially when the dire consequences are somewhere in the future. However, some of the disregard must be charged to conflicting information from official sources, which, if technical, confuses rather than informs the lay reader. Often the lengthening litany of dangers to health leads to the conclusion that inasmuch as "everything is dangerous," it is best to do as one likes and ignore them all. There is also vacillation between growing lists of dangers to health and the optimistic reports about advances in medicine that will either obviate or cure the effects of these dangers. A general distrust of official agencies, including organized medicine, does not help the situation.

Polls taken by the Louis Harris organization in 1966 and again early in 1977 found that public confidence in the executive branch of the federal government had slipped from 41 percent to 23 percent; confidence in Congress had gone from 42 percent to 17 percent; and confidence in organized medicine had ebbed from 73 percent to 43 percent.

Like technological overload, the absolute amount of information available to the citizen on every important issue and in every department of life is probably greater than it has been in recorded history. Never have so many people been told so much about so many different things. Yet never has the volume of the unknown, indeterminate, and problematical been greater.

Information overload affects both the quantity of information and the conceptual demands it makes on the reader. Most of the citizenry should be able to use the basic concepts studied in the standard academic subjects usually prescribed for general education to interpret information on various topics. Many college graduates have not had much more than a smattering of such general studies. Some have not taken this or that science; some have had bits of a few social sciences, and a few stray courses in the humanities. But even when general education has been adequate, the literature to which the citizen has to react is not likely to be written for the generalist.

One scientist, commenting on the difficulty of conveying scientific findings to the layman, noted:

> In my capacity as scientist, I am quite often in court as an expert witness. As such I can express opinions, as well as testify as to fact. Usually I am asked to do so by counsel who have retained me. Most times I can only answer part of his questions, even when they've been rehearsed. When I am cross-examined, opposing counsel continues the process—and then puts on his own expert, with credentials at least as good as mine, who says just the reverse of what I said. The judge shakes his head, scribbles notes on his pad, and clearly makes that same lay judgment: he's incompetent![2]

The specialized languages of academic and professional guilds render even college graduates functionally illiterate.

SIMPLISTIC AND COMPLEX SOLUTIONS

Citizen A reads in the daily press, in news magazines, and in journals devoted to business that inflation is caused by too many dollars chasing too few goods. This makes sense to Mr. A as an example of supply and demand determining price. However, it occurs to Mr. A to ask, if this is a proper explanation of inflation, then why are the newspapers full of advertising urging consumers to buy "scarce" goods? Either there is an adequate supply of goods, inasmuch as merchants are spending money to get rid of them, or they are luring consumers to bid up the price of scarce goods. And doesn't the cost of advertising raise the price even more?

A customer finds an article on the supermarket shelf with three prices and the two lower ones crossed out. He objects that the prices should not have been raised because the original cost to the dealer had remained the same. Was not this an example of gouging?

Inasmuch as the experts say that inflation is fueled by a spiraling of prices and costs, the ordinary citizen naturally thinks that the spiral can be stopped by putting a lid on prices and wages.

These and kindred musings are rejected by the economic *cognoscenti* as simplistic thinking. The real explanation is far more complex, Mr. A is told. Since economists do not agree on a complex explanation, Mr. A concludes, not without reason, that if there are no simple solutions, there are no complex ones either.

> *Item*: During a period in which beef prices rose sharply in supermarkets, consumers staged a boycott of sorts, presumably to bring the price down by creating an oversupply. The cattlemen responded with the threat that if the prices did go down as a result of the boycott, they would reduce their herds so that in the end prices would go up even more.

In other words, if consumers chase the goods, prices go up; if they don't chase, they go up.

> *Item*: The *Wall Street Journal* unequivocally blames inflation on the government's "printing money" to meet its deficits. This creates too many dollars chasing too few goods.

Mr. A asks: "Don't American Express, Visa, Master Charge, as well as the banks, create credit that makes for more dollars chasing fewer goods? Isn't that also printing money? Why not put a stop to printing credit cards?" This, we were told, is a simplistic answer, albeit it was finally given a try in the latter days of 1979 and seemed to work so well that it threatened to reduce consumer spending well below what the consumer goods industries would tolerate. Mr. A can be forgiven if he wonders: "If the simple solutions are false, are there any solutions at all?"

Economics is not alone in this bind. All the social sciences suffer from an inability to use the methods of the physical sciences to arrive at causal explanations. They have little agreement on how many and which variables are relevant, and they can rarely set up experiments that approximate the conditions of the real world. As a result, they have to be satisfied with correlations that may or may not reveal causes. When a society is plagued by problems, however, its members want causes so that they can take rational remedial action, not conjectures wrapped in probable and improbable errors.

There is a sense also that economics, like military science, and business administration are not purely descriptive in intent. Each of these is a helping "science" designed to arrive at the best system of economic activities, the most likely to achieve military victories, the organization that will ensure the maximum efficiency. The goal of the study is not primarily to describe existing practices and detect the laws underlying them for their own sake, although they often sound as if that were their goal, but rather to use the generalizations to prescribe meliorative strategies. These disciplines arise out of practical situations and are of not much interest to the public apart from them. It is little wonder, therefore, that the citizen expects the economic analyst and theoretician to prescribe what will produce the maximum of goods and services for his social order.

On a quite different plane, the "simplistic" label could be applied pejoratively to the following remarks attributed to Dwight D. Eisenhower, made on 16 April 1953, before the American Society of Newspaper Editors:

> Every gun that is made, every warship launched, every rocket fired signifies in the final sense, a theft from those who hunger and are not fed, those who are cold and are not clothed. This world in arms is not spending money alone. It is spending the sweat of its laborers, the genius of its scientists, the hopes of its children. . . . This is not a way of life at all in any true sense. Under the cloud of threatening war, it is humanity hanging on a cross of iron.[3]

Clearly, this is not the technical analysis of an expert on military affairs, and it is safe to conjecture that Dear Abby used it because it was not. It was a simple and direct reaction to war by a military figure who chose to talk in ordinary language, and it probably outraged the economists as well as the experts in the military strategy think tanks as simplistic. Once more, if this simplistic solution is to be rejected, what complicated and sophisticated one is to take its place?

The examples of the fallacy of "misplaced simplicity" or "misplaced complexity" could be multiplied, and when people get together they do multiply them into long lists of what seem to be mindless anomalies. Why, wonders the traveler standing in a long line in front of an airline ticket counter, does one have to wait 20 minutes in order to find out whether a flight taking off in 20 minutes has available space? Why, one wonders, must the request for information that would take one minute to answer wait until the clerk has solved a complicated situation that will take 15 minutes to unravel? Why, the naive public wonders, are not cases that all parties announce will be appealed to the U.S. Supreme Court not tried in the Supreme Court in the first place?

At this point it may be useful to distinguish between problems and their solutions, on the one hand, and predicaments and escaping from them, on the other. A predicament is an uncomfortable situation in which action is frustrated. A flat tire, on the way to an important appointment, is first experienced as a predicament, a pickle. If a friendly passing motorist offers a lift, the predicament is eased; if the friendly motorist then flourishes a gun and demands money, a new predicament is created. Neither predicament becomes a problem until one wishes to extricate himself from it by rational methods, that is, by methods that follow from an understanding of the causes of the predicament and the formulation of hypotheses as to probable solutions. Thus Dewey's CAT begins with a predicament, a felt difficulty, rather than a problem, and if a reflex action, a well-established habit or a random movement relieves the situation, there is no need for thinking. A problem is a predicament trussed up for inquiry. A solution is a rationally grounded relief of a predicament; and when we say there are no simple solutions, it may mean that our theoretical resources for fruitful hypotheses are bankrupt and that only *ad hoc* hypotheses to account for a multitude of apparently discrete factors are available.

The principle of parsimony in the logic of science is witness to the presumptive importance of simplicity, especially if the difference between psychological and logical simplicity is observed. As a science advances, its theories become logically simpler, albeit not always psychologically so.[4]

PITFALLS OF PLANNING

Nothing so epitomizes the rational approach to action as planning. Planning means foreseeing goals, careful contriving of suitable means, and assessing possible consequences. Planning is the opposite of acting on impulse, custom, tradition, and other irrational or nonrational motivations. It follows that a rational society would be a planning and planned society. In democratic societies the amount of planning by the government is the subject of constant debate. In socialist countries sound doctrine urges the government to plan everything. Libertarians balk at the government planning anything. In totalitarian countries the machinery for planning is easier to install and maintain, although it is sometimes difficult to distinguish planning from arbitrary control.

As a society becomes complex and its variables intertwine, a little planning is dangerous and total planning is futile. Too little or partial planning is dangerous because the unplanned areas will disrupt or be disrupted.[5] Corporations plan their activities very carefully but object to social planning by the government. Organized labor is a challenge to organized industry, and unorganized labor is a threat to organized labor.

As for total planning, under present conditions, it is simply impossible. The broader and more encompassing the plan, the more vulnerable it becomes to serendipity (unexpected good luck) and its opposite, what might be dubbed diremipity (unexpected bad luck). Too many persons, too many human errors, too many mechanical failures—all conspire to make the outcome of the planned activity highly conjectural. For example, in one of the recent oil crises, the National Energy Board planned to store oil in some worked-out salt mines in Louisiana. Extensive and intensive planning marshaled extensive and intensive expertise. No expense was spared. But it turned into a huge bungle because too many agencies were involved, too many factors and people had to be coordinated, and too many variables were operating over which the planners seemed to have no control. A national television program portrayed the "fiasco" to a public cringing from the effects of inflation, government expenditures, fuel shortages, and crises. It did little to strengthen the faith of the public in planning.

The same sort of obstacles frustrate attempts to order individual life rationally, and the frustration is no less galling for being the result of a thousand trivial events that "just happen" to collide and jostle the best-laid plans into comical disarray. This does not mean that planning is always futile, but it does mean that the scope of reliable planning is severely limited to situations that are reasonably self-contained and in which the relevant variables can be estimated and controlled. Such situations are not easy to find; big plans invite futility, and overorganizing little ones smacks of a trivializing fussiness; careful investment of time and thought into situations of intermediate scale seems to be the sensible, albeit pedestrian, compromise.

Not the least of the obstacles to planning are its own verities: orderliness, system, predictability. These are the characteristics of establishments. Although they reduce uncertainty and ambiguity, to free creative spirits, they institutionalize boredom, stupidity, and unwarranted repression of freedom. Hence, while eager students spent hours on hours organizing protests and planning to bring down the establishments, they did so, they said, in order to free their own lives from planned conformity. Their parents counted on planned conformity for peace of mind. Substituting impulse for planning became a slogan for many young people in the late 1960s and early '70s. In the latter years of the 1970s, as middle-agers they manifested a tendency to be orderly about their jobs and less so about other phases of life. Today all ages are given reams of advice on how to liberate themselves from excess order.

In any event, the student sit-ins and protest movements of the turbulent decades taught us all how vulnerable a complex system is to disruption by interference with one of its interlocking subsystems. A university could be paralyzed by a sit-in at the administration building or by leaving telephone receivers off hooks. A piece of paper with writing or printing properly inserted into the administrative apparatus, for example, ensures its immortality: somebody in the system would have to read it, respond to it, refer it, and at the very least file it. Petitions, resolutions, memoranda could choke the system.

RANDOMIZATION OF GOOD AND EVIL

Rational action requires that good and evil be distributed according to some intelligible principle so that action can be planned and chosen selectively. Granted that the density of events and the impenetrable jungle of consequences prevent orderly landscaping of the moral estate, total dissociation of action from just deserts paralyzes the thoughtful human being. What happens in a society when the incidence of good and evil approach randomization? Consider the following news item:

> Corydon and Arden Sperry, whose 21-year-old son was shot to death in their Bedford Hills home last May along with the family's longtime governess, identified in State Supreme Court furs, jewelry and other items allegedly taken from their home in the course of the murders. . . .
>
> Christopher Sperry was shot the night of last May 9 along with 82-year-old Nellie McCormack, the former governess, and two neighbors, Dr. and Mrs. Charles Frankel. Dr. Frankel was a philosophy professor at Columbia University and a former assistant Secretary of State.

Although the death of Professor Frankel was no more tragic than the deaths of the others and no more intelligible, the irony of a professor of philosophy who in doctrine and life put a high premium on rational action becoming a victim of what must be called randomized evil cannot escape notice.

Who will be mugged or raped or robbed or struck down by a motor vehicle is not even a matter of calculable probability. Earthquakes, floods, fires, oil spills, plagues and pollution, like street criminals, fall on the just and unjust alike. The increase of "senseless" crime is not causeless. Social scientists and the police are busy seeking its causes in social factors and psychologists in individual ones. It is rational to seek causal explanations, but not necessarily to plan one's daily life on them. The more qualifications a generalization or explanatory formula must make, the less useful it is for prediction in individual cases; and it is individual cases that interest the individual. The inability to foretell whether one is to be in the group covered by the generalization or fall into one of its numerous exceptions randomizes the consequences of choice and action.

The randomization of the incidence of good and evil deflates the importance of planning and rational action in general, on the one hand, and on the other, promotes the cocoon syndrome. In this syndrome, one builds protection against a multiplicity of possible evils by cutting as many ties to others and to fortune as possible. It separates individuals despite their proximity in apartment complexes and on the job. It can take the form of physical separation with locks and bolts to keep everyone, including possible evildoers, out. It may take the form of flight from the inner city into a presumably safer suburb or even to a remote farm or island. Or it can drive the fearful ones into taking out insurance on fire, water, wind, auto collisions, aircraft mishaps, burglary, and professional malpractice. To make sure the insurance policies will pay off, one—of course—takes out another policy to cover this contingency also.

A more subtle but no less pervasive cocoon reaction is indifference. What is one to do when surrounded by persons who are defying one's deeply felt norms of right and wrong, decent and indecent? And what is one to do when it is no longer fashionable to be indignant about such unconventional attitudes and behavior? One response, and perhaps the most plausible one, is withdrawal. One stays away from motion pictures of which one disapproves, or refuses to associate with persons who indulge in sexual practices that disturb one's sense of propriety.

For genuine indifference, however, a rigorous deconditioning would be required to break the affective connections with certain norms of behavior, a process akin to desensitizing oneself to certain allergenic agents. This is hard to achieve without regulated exposure to the very behavior to which one would like to become indifferent—perhaps in small amounts to begin with, with increasing dosage. Thus one might first become indifferent or learn to tolerate persons who are "living in sin" in fairly well ordered households and gradually achieve tolerance to people who practice group sex or indulge in sadomasochistic practices. Of course, there is the danger that such exposure might turn to liking. Hence the weird incoherence of an age that at one and the same time shrieks for liberation *from* and caring *for* others. Freedom from the judgment of others legitimates their indifference to us. We can't have it both ways.

A highly philosophical cocoon is that of the Stoic. According to Marcus Aurelius, the Roman emperor who was also a famous Stoic, "Everything harmonizes with me which is harmonious to thee, O Universe. Nothing for me is too early nor too late, which is in due time for thee. Everything is fruit to me, which the seasons bring, O Nature: from thee are all things, in thee are all things, to thee all things return."

Stoicism is the stance in which one becomes impervious to external evils by cultivated indifference to pleasure and pain. The virtuous man and woman can, by realizing their unity with Nature, preserve intellectual and moral integrity despite the pressure of the passions and vagaries of external circumstances. Stoicism is one way of rising above the randomization of good and evil and that a Roman emperor and a slave (Epictetus) both saw their salvation in it says something to a society in which a wide range of individuals are seeking to come to terms with factors over which they seem to have little or no control.

The cocoon syndrome is a protective, not a progressive, device. It is not reformative or activist with respect to society. To some it may even be an immoral option, yet on strictly prudential grounds, is it an unreasonable one?

The randomization of the incidence of good and evil is not prevented or substantially mitigated by advances in technology. Technology, for example, has not reduced the incidence of street crime nor made it more risky for the criminal. In the realms of health, technology has had more success, although it has also facilitated the migration of bacteria and viruses across continents so that every visit to an international airport is a potential, albeit a low, risk of infection.

Nor can technological advance be taken as evidence for the increased intelligence of the public, an increase that might be expected to reduce the randomization of the incidence of good and evil. High technology can coexist with a diminution as well as increase of mind. Sophisticated technology can be used day in and day out without understanding how it works; indeed, the glory of modern technology is greatest when its demand on the intelligence of the user is least. This is one reason the claim that a modern society demands a high order of schooling is only partially true. The society must generate enough educational resources to supply the need for upper-level personnel to invent and administer the technology, but not every worker or user needs this level of understanding.[6]

Indeed, one of the measures of good technology is the degree to which its users do not have to understand it. A good example of good technology is the electric refrigerator. Not only does it cool foods efficiently and reliably; but it does so automatically. The decisional demand on the user is reduced to turning a dial and inserting the plug into an outlet. The user does not have to understand the theory of electricity nor the intricate processes by which gases are compressed and expanded to extract heat from air at room temperature. This example could be multiplied to make up a long list. A child can put an electric utility in motion. What happens to the adaptive powers of individual minds as the cognitive strain upon them is relieved by machines that embody intelligence, what may be called a technologized intelligence? One answer is that individual minds can now turn their attention to non-technological problems, but what if the steady advance of technology forms the habit of expecting all problems to be solved by a mechanized mind? No, collective mind is not necessarily the sum of its individual minds. High technology and diminished mind can go together.

One result of having to face these obstacles to rational action is a distrust of social institutions. Groups tend to organize for narrow interests; individuals retreat into their cocoons. The narcissism of the past decade has been blamed for the distrust, but feelings of impotence in affecting social policy may have driven many into narcissism. About health fads, the exercise craze, the development of personal power by cults and healers too diverse to list, literature and film that celebrate Self, there is an aura of panic, an uneasy fear that it is everyone for himself.

Many of the examples cited above were topics of grim humor in the last decade. The *litterati* and pundits on the Left had a picnic with the oddities and apparent insanities of the current culture. The counterculture erected a metaphysic and ethic on them. The theater of the absurd made its points using similar materials. All of which does not prove that the world is absurd, but leaves little doubt that the public is more than half ready to believe that it is, and perhaps has to be.

However, the absurd is only so against a background of expectations that there is or can be a rational world. Celebration of the absurd, therefore, has been a standard form of exposing it. Comedy and farce are entertaining ways of preaching social sermons. Delight in the absurd for its own sake has an amusing childish quality, but when used to escape from the constraints of rationality borders on mental pathology. Contrived zaniness in entertainment media and books that string together fantasies and *non sequiturs* create more absurdity than they reveal. They really are absurd!

There would be little point in reiterating the foibles and pratfalls of our culture if the walls between comedy and tragedy were not so thin and fragile. Idiocies in the bureaucracy are funny until they result in a nuclear accident or runaway inflation or an atomic war. What is one to call a catastrophe caused by an absent-minded clerk punching the wrong button? That is why pointing out the failure of planning, the randomization of good and evil, and the like are not merely "cheap shots," as the saying goes, for a quick laugh. For they may be signals that the absurd is turning into tragedy. I am reminded of a passage in one of Søren Kierkegaard's books in which two friends meet, and one invites the other to his home for dinner on a certain date. The invited guest thinks for several moments and in all seriousness replies somewhat as follows: "Yes, I shall be glad to come and I shall be there, provided that on the way a roof tile does not fall and kill me." In a world where events occur with dependable probability, such a remark strikes us as incongruous and even unhealthy. For Kierkegaard, this absurdity served by indirect communication to convey seriousness, a sense of the precariousness of existence. Suppose that the invited guest had said that he would be glad to come to dinner and that he would be there at the appointed time, if on the way he were not attacked by hoodlums and taken to the hospital instead. Is this, in our time in many sections of our large cities, to be taken as an incongruous and unhealthy reservation?[7]

Today the lack of control over the circumstances of life goes hand in hand with our enormously increased understanding of and control over the physical environment. It is not the waywardness of nature but the waywardness and limitations of human beings that frustrate the anticipation and control of the future by rational planning. In such circumstances it is difficult to make a decent tragedy out of our frustrations; at best, it is a comedy that is not really funny. At worst, it can become a fatal farce.

All of which makes the relation of truth as the aggregate of warranted assertions to rational action problematic. Knowledge so considered may be rational and yet frustrate rational action. To serve action, knowledge has to be organized differently than for inquiry. It has to become part of the texture of practical reasoning with its chain of purposes and consequences. It has to meet the test of credibility as well as truth.

REFERENCES

1. William Graham Sumner, *Folkways* (New York: Dover, 1959), first published in 1906. While the Social Darwinism of this work repelled the disciples of the Enlightenment, it still serves as a stark reminder of the marginal role of thought and reason in the ordinary conduct of life.

2. F.K. Hare, "Uncertainties in the Physical World," in *Man and His Environment*, ed. M.F. Mohtade (New York: Pergamon Press, 1980), 3: 68.

3. Abigail Van Buren, reprinted in *Dear Abby*, 6 September 1980.

4. One is reminded in this connection of Henri Bergson's doctrine that the evolution of living things must have been the result of a single original creative *élan vital*. Only when the human intellect tries to conceptualize it does it become bewilderingly complex. Intellect, said Bergson, has to analyze; only intuition can grasp the creative thrust as such. Of course, Charles Darwin, using his intellect, succeeded in developing a theory that helped bring the complexity within the scope of understanding.

5. This is not a recent problem. Karl Mannheim was concerned about the coexistence of planned and unplanned activities within a society. *Man and Society in an Age of Reconstruction* (New York: Harcourt, Brace 1940), pp. 155 ff.

6. H.S. Broudy, "Science, Technology, and the Diminished Mind," the Ninth Damon Lecture, *Journal of College Science Teaching*, 5 no. 5 (May 1976): 292–96.

7. H.S. Broudy, "Kierkegaard on Indirect Communication," *Journal of Philosophy* 58 (1961): 225–33.

4

Obstacles to Belief

In the previous chapter an assortment of situations and circumstances that impede rational action were listed. These obstacles seem to be thrown up by the complexity of factors and their interdependence. The complexity strains our data processing technology, advanced though it is, while the interdependence balks our efforts at analysis, diagnosis, and remediation. Further advances in electronic technology, no doubt, will improve our ability to cope with complexity, but interdependence poses difficulties that go beyond the quantity and diversity of data.

Just as successful surgery requires the excision of the diseased tissue without destroying the surrounding nerves and blood vessels, so conceptualizing a problem requires delicate delimitation. Only in this way can we come to understand a phenomenon, that is, the way in which its elements are related to each other. Before computers can handle more variables, the variables have to be identified and conceptually distinguished from each other. If an interconnecting network of meanings defies such sorting out, however, then as the Absolute Idealists held, we cannot understand anything without understanding everything. And if the interconnections among the activities of human beings cannot be separated conceptually without doing violence to their existential integrity, dealing with the world rationally seems an unpromising prospect.

The citizen gets information and advice from scholars in the various disciplines (located in the university), professionals who apply some of the disciplinary knowledge in order to serve their clientele (law, medicine, engineering, architecture, etc.) and from officials (recruited from the academy and the professions) who administer the social, governmental, and corporate institutions.

This information and advice come to the citizenry through professional services, their own studies in formal schooling, and pronouncements in the mass media emanating, sought and unsought, from bureaus, commissions, learned societies, essayists, and commentators. These are the sources of what is supposed to be the most reliable available knowledge. If these sources are regarded as untrustworthy because of lack of competence or lack of character, the potential for rational action by the citizenry is seriously diminished.

Competence is always relevant. When experts cannot agree on analyses and remedies of important problems, such as crime, drug abuse, cancer, poverty, the control of armaments, and inflation, the competence of the experts is bound to be called into question. Furthermore, not all the sciences are equally precise in their formulations and application. The social sciences have difficulty maintaining a claim to the title of science; the theoretical base for social work, education, or politics cannot compare in rigor with that available to medicine, agriculture, or engineering.

The moderately well educated citizen does not, I believe, ignore these differences in the state of the arts and sciences. Nor does he routinely expect simple and quick solutions to complex problems. Nevertheless, when a vast array of experts day after day, year after year, use their scholarly apparatus to show that certain social problems elude their best efforts, it is hard to blame the citizen for tuning them out altogether.

Perhaps the most glaring example of learned impotence is furnished by the confraternity of economists, whether they are located in the university, the government, industry, or on Wall Street. Their difficulties will be discussed in some detail in chapter 6 because of their impact on society as a whole, but they could be matched in other fields that try to use the methods of social science to describe, explain, and prescribe for social problems.

SPECIALISM

Another source of skepticism with respect to the guiding potential of organized knowledge is the ever increasing specialization among scholars and professionals. Nothing is more familiar to modern society than specialization. It is the key to mass production of commodities and, therefore, to the economic enterprise. It exemplifies the principle that efficiency requires exclusive attention to operations of very limited scope. Specialization is a feature not only of large-scale machine production but of the professions and of virtually all our institutions.

Specialization can make diametrically opposite demands on the powers of the worker. For example, a task can be so finely subdivided that the skill and knowledge needed to perform it is reduced to what a near-idiot can muster. On the other hand, specialization in, let us say, neuro-surgery increases the cognitive demands beyond that needed by the general practitioner. Specialism, while theoretically promising to improve efficiency, may in practice do the opposite, and instead of increasing the credibility of the specialist, may reduce it. The counterproductivity of specialism comes from (1) the narrowness of the specialist's interest, which runs counter to the more concrete interest of the layperson, and (2) the tendency of specialism to substitute procedures for substance.

Specialization means separating out an activity from the network of interdependence, and in knowledge such separation is indispensable. For one thing, to make good its claims to objectivity and impartiality, intellectual inquiry must abstract from (separate from) all noncognitive factors. The wishes of the investigator, psychological strains and stresses, the adventures of discovery, and a host of other interesting circumstances must be trimmed, separated from the content of the proposition that is put forward as true (i.e., as a warranted assertion). The biography of inquiry has to be kept distinct from the content and method of inquiry.

Furthermore, the entities, relations, and theories of one domain have to be kept distinct from those of other domains. Each domain develops an internal logic, modes of inquiry, and canons of evidence. Efforts at relating different disciplines come late in the game and are not undertaken lightly by workers within the several disciplines or professions. Inter- or multidisciplinary studies are threats to disciplinary specialism upon which academic status within the guild of the discipline depends. Interdisciplinary study entails the logical relating of the concepts of two or more disciplines; multidisciplinary work occurs when a problem such as environmental pollution draws upon the concepts of more than a single discipline. Accordingly, we encounter such slogans as business is business, law is not justice, euthanasia is not a medical problem, the pollution of the environment is not a problem for the chemical industry, and so forth. Walls are built around the selected field of inquiry or practice, and everything outside the walls is challenged to prove its relevance when it tries to enter into the discussion.

However, the citizen cannot cut himself or the society in which he has to live into distinct segments. The various value domains foam over into each other. Health values; recreational values; the values of various forms of social relationships; the intellectual, religious, aesthetic, and moral values; however we distinguish them in thought, they reverberate together. It is not surprising, therefore, that the citizen finds the "business is business" dictum incredible, and regards those who argue that a court decision is "good law" but poor justice as amoral if not immoral. Furthermore, as specialism grows, the moral dimension becomes nobody's business—except, of course, every citizen's.

The tension between the need to free a field of inquiry from the context of life and the implicit resistance of the citizen to such a separation plagues all modes of intellectual inquiry and professional practice. In large part it is rooted in the positivistic doctrine that descriptive propositions can and should be distinguished sharply from evaluational ones.

Suppose, for example, the proposition that it is safe and economical to build nuclear reactors is asserted by (1) an executive in the Environmental Protection Agency, (2) the president of a utility company, and (3) the Russian ambassador. If we separate the cognitive from the noncognitive factors, then the truth of the assertion has nothing to do with the identity of the speakers or their motives for uttering the statement. As a description of a state of affairs, it is the same statement uttered by three different speakers. But what is the state of affairs that is being described? Is it the same for all three?

For the citizen there are three states of affairs, not one, and each includes the identity of the speaker, which is an indicator of an interest in having the statement accepted by the public. If the citizen can verify the statement "nuclear reactors are safe" on scientific and technological criteria, *who* makes the statement is a matter of indifference; but if he cannot do so—and usually he cannot—*who* makes it and *why* may make all the difference. Clearly, the credibility of the statement is enhanced more by the EPA representative's assent than by that of the other two. But what if the EPA representative had denied that the "facts show nuclear reactors to be safe"? Here the grounds for credibility become murky, because a variety of motives are involved. Nevertheless, who stands to profit, *cui bono*, will be a relevant factor.

Whether there are purely descriptive utterances or sayings that are not also doings (speech acts) is an interesting question. Even reporting that the "facts show that nuclear reactors are safe" is not done alone in a desert. It is also an act of communication made in order to explain, reassure, persuade the listener or reader. The difference between truth and credibility is that the intent of a warranted assertion is to reveal or explain so that the recipient can understand, grasp, comprehend, whereas credibility has to do with the persuasive effect the utterance will have on the hearer's commitment.[1]

LINGUISTIC AND PROCEDURAL MASKS

Specialism affects the credibility of specialists, be they scholars, professionals, or officials, in at least two ways. One is through the effect of highly technical and esoteric terminology. One man's technical language is another's jargon and by implication an unnecessary obfuscation. As a result, when a culture multiplies its specialties, more and more of what the citizen hears is heard as jargon meant to conceal and confuse. The current spate of legislation mandating the use of ordinary language in commercial contracts and consumer warranties is evidence of this phenomenon and the lack of credibility it engenders.

The other way, or *an* other way, that specialism affects credibility is by its stress on procedures. When, for example, a citizen complains that an article he purchased is defective or that his property has not been assessed equitably, he is directed to a complicated set of procedures that promise to route his complaints to the proper persons who will institute other procedures that will activate other proper persons, and so on, and so on. The citizen to whom the cause of the complaint and its remedy seem to be a straightforward affair can hardly be blamed for believing that the required procedures are unnecessary, baffling, and designed to frustrate him and to discourage further complaints. These suspicions are confirmed when "action lines" operated by radio and television stations cut through the procedures and get results in an amazingly short time.

To the layperson the substantive issue is whether the defendant is guilty or innocent, whether the measure before the legislature is just or not; whether the store will refund the purchase price of an unsatisfactory product. Formalized procedures are defended on the ground that they efficiently and reliably produce uniform and presumably fair treatment to all parties; that they ensure against subjective idiosyncrasies of judgment, and, above all, because they provide a system of accounting. Failure to follow the rules of procedure is *prima facie* blameworthy; following them is a *prima facie* defense against complaints. It should be noted that in one's own field of specialization (where one is not a layperson), elaborate rules are usually accepted as necessary; in fields outside one's field of expertise, their necessity and beneficence are not so obvious.

In the mind of the citizen, the suspicion is planted and grows that procedures are diversions contrived for the benefit of those who conduct them. For example, the more elaborate the procedures interposed between the poor and the benefits legislated for their relief, the less likely the benefits will be received by those who deserve them, and the more likely that they will be siphoned off by the shrewd, unscrupulous operator who uses the procedures to his advantage. Make the registration and voting process sufficiently complex, and the percentage voting goes down among the very citizens who have the most to lose by not exercising the franchise. That the procedures of governmental agencies provide jobs for its employees is clear; that they produce social benefits is open to question.

The suspicions of the lay public may be unfounded, although the number of "action lines" operated by radio and television stations and the persistent efforts to demystify the procedures of law, government, and commerce by consumer groups argue to the contrary. There comes a time in the life of an organization or institution when the maintenance of the procedures becomes an end and even a field of specialization in itself. In principle, there is no limit to the invention of procedures to monitor other procedures that in turn monitor procedures. Some operations and institutions of government are reaching this stage of absurdity, which to the layperson becomes obvious long before it reaches the consciousness of organizational specialists and professional bureaucrats. To the latter the procedures turn into intricate games that are worth playing for their own sake; to the lay citizen, however, this is plain wrongheaded and indicative of an attempt to evade the substantive issues.[2]

Not only does procedural complexity obey Parkinson's law to fill all available time at the disposal of the administrative cadres, but it also provides the bureaucrat with a way of avoiding difficult decisions and taking responsibility for them. The technique is simple and familiar. Elaborate the decision-making machinery by instituting as many review boards as possible; increase the number of participants; keep the discussion going until sheer pressure of circumstance forces some sort of compromise for which the leadership (or anyone else) cannot be blamed. Much of the enthusiasm for participatory democracy emanates from the moral axiom that it is only right and fair that those who are involved in the consequences of a policy or measure should have a voice in deciding on what shall be done. Participatory democracy is a prime preventive of arbitrary decisions by authorities, but it is also a way by which leaders can evade their responsibility for making any decisions.

Of all the distortions that specialism and the insistence on limited spheres of relevance produce, the most vital to the citizen is the bracketing of the moral dimension. The categories of duty, rights, obligation, fairness, and justice are embedded in the mores of every society; formal education may refine these categories, but it does not originate them. The specialized disciplines and professions lose credibility when the question Is it fair? Is it just? is ruled out of order. Thus the separation of the question whether the accused has been proved guilty (even if he has confessed) from the injuries sustained by the victim seems to the citizen grossly immoral, but to the courts a necessary distinction. Not all the lawyers in the nation can convince a consumer who has been cheated that the lack of a written contract should protect the cheater, and the victim of a rape or robbery will never be reconciled to the acquittal of the accused because of legal technicalities.

LANGUAGE, TRUTH, AND CREDIBILITY

Both truth and credibility have an intimate, albeit somewhat different, dependence on language. Propositional truth, especially the kind called warranted assertion about matters of fact, is stated in the language of conceptual systems, which map the area of inquiry and direct the proper modes of investigation.

Language affects the meaning of assertions by its natural ambiguities, but also by deliberate distortions. Thus the "wretched poor" does not convey the same import as "socially and economically disadvantaged," and a "defensive withdrawal" not the same as "retreat." The euphemism invites assent, which might not be given to the original meaning.

The distortion is carried to extremes when by linguistic devices the meaning of a term is given a turn of 180 degrees, when writers say that madness is a form of knowledge and the sane are the truly mad ones, when the terrorist is presented as the victim, and the like.[3] The sentence "The inmates of the insane asylum are the only truly sane members of our society" is grammatically correct, and nothing prevents the combining of these words in this way. The paradoxes are accepted because they make grammatical sense.

What happens when such manipulations of language are translated into a tool for social criticism? The citizen may well ask, "Why is language being used to charge that insane asylums have detained the wrong patients?" Or he may ask whether grammatical correctness warrants the conclusion that terrorists are really the victims and not those whose blood they shed. How much of academic social ideology is the result of intoxication with the possibilities of language? If there is a word, it is a temptation to invent a "reality" to match it. Such play with ideas and language is harmless when confined to the intellectual games that academics play and have been authorized by society to play; but when they are used to incite political action, the citizen is entitled to know what motivates the scholars. How sincere are these pronouncements? What risk do they take by making them?

In older and more benighted times, dissenting intellectuals were sometimes burned at the stake for their beliefs. In more recent times, they have been detained in mental hospitals and harassed by police, and it has become fashionable recently in some quarters of the globe liberated by revolution to threaten them with the cutting of hands and perhaps tongues. Under such invitations to martyrdom it is not difficult to distinguish the genuine commitment from the imitation; but when intellectuals are protected from such harsh credibility tests by freedom of speech, tenure, and relative affluence, credibility cannot be taken for granted. They must create it and protect it themselves. During the 1960s, for example, the credibility of revolutionary students and academics with the workers for whom they were presumably demonstrating was brutally low.

PERSONS, THINGS, SUBJECTS, OBJECTS

Nevertheless, not all ambiguous, figurative, and even perverse uses of language are false, trivial, or useless. Language, one must suppose, came into being fairly early in the evolutionary game; to translate particular images of objects into verbal symbols was a giant step forward. Like images, words gain their extraordinary importance from their separability from the objects to which they refer. Once so freed, they can be combined by the imagination and later by conceptual thought in virtual independence of the actual world. This is the source of man's truth and error, of every ideal and debasement. By it man can create a realm of reality, and it is no pun to say that he creates it "literally."

Language and the other media of the imagination create possibility. The reiterative and reflexive nature of language makes it possible for the mind to envisage unlimited extrapolation of whatever good or evil it contemplates. It can invent by imagination unlimited pleasures and the tortures of hell. Art creates images of possible feeling just as the intellect can create systems of possible thought, and with luck the artist's images can be both knowledgeful feeling and feelingful knowledge at one and the same time.

Once possibility is brought into being and expanded by the human mind, the problem of truth becomes acute. Which of the apparitions and possibilities are real and which are no more than figments of the imagination? Reality is a problem because language and imagery can produce appearances that purport to be the appearance of something more than mere appearance. No wholly satisfactory criterion of the real has been produced by philosophy, as Descartes' efforts give witness; for Descartes in search of certainty, only a credible and honest supernatural power could warrant that human minds would not be wholly and permanently deceived.

Yet we do have criteria. Permanence, resistance to external influence, and resistance to our wishes are some of them. The real persists and exerts influence while more or less resisting the influence of other entities. On these criteria, some of the creations of the human mind—beliefs, aspirations, ideals, standards—are real indeed. To be sure, there is another and most important test, namely, scientific verification, which is a sophisticated way of making as sure as one can be that the nature of the objects under investigation are not mere figments of the imagination or subjective projections of wishes or the product of wild hypotheses. Yet only the most insensitive and irreconcilable positivist would restrict reality to what can be described and explained in literal, empirically verifiable referential language.

There is a reality—on the criteria mentioned—that comes into being because human minds imagine a state of affairs that they are willing to accept as a commitment. And whether or not that reality exists in the positivistic, empirical sense, a life led as if an ideal were real is different from one from which this faith is absent. It is the kind of being that becomes actual by virtue of what William James called the "will to believe." Two kinds of being fill the human stage: the array of things that comprise the physical world, from cells to galaxies, and persons who comprise not only bodies as cells, but embodied images of what is and might be.

The language that communicates these two kinds of being is not the same, and I believe it makes sense to speak of existential language as differing from scientific language. To no small extent, the difference between truth and credibility is isomorphic with this distinction. One philosopher has stated the distinction in this way:

> Within the scientific framework [the truth], persons are construed as complex systems of logical subjects. They are systems of physical entities of the same "stuff" as rocks, trees, chairs, and tables. . . . Hence persons have no distinct identity. They are merely complex arrangements of more basic ontological units. On the other hand, within the framework of the mental, persons are taken as indivisible telic entities, distinct from inanimate nature. They alone are the logical subjects of intentions, motives, and indeed a whole array of "entities" which they are said to "have" and which cause them to act as they do. . . . what is a distinct, separable event to one framework may not be on the other.[4]

Even rocks can have distinct identity, if one takes the trouble to label the peculiarities of weight, size, shape, and the like that individuate them. The specimens collected and displayed in the museum are individual things, not just things. Nevertheless, these individuating data are the least important and interesting features about them. Suppose, however, one were to find the stone that David shot at Goliath. Much intellectual effort might have been expended to show that in fact *this* was the stone. No other stone could then replace it in historical fact and significance, albeit 10,000 stones of similar size and composition could be found. One might speculate that the importance of *this* stone would lie in its power to help persons recollect and reconstruct the past, but it is the past of David and the circumstances of its use that makes it significant, not its size and chemical composition. It is not a telic entity.

When we ask about the truth as regards persons, the epistemological situation changes radically, if it is the case that ". . . within the framework of the mental, persons are taken as indivisible telic entities distinct from inanimate nature. They alone are the logical subjects of intentions, motives, and indeed a whole array of 'entities' which they are said to 'have' and which cause them to act as they do. . . ." What then is the truth about persons? Is it the reporting of the whole array of such entities? If so, it makes sense to think of truth here as subjective, that is of what is important to a subject, indeed, that which constitutes that subject.

If we say that proposition P is credible, we mean that the evidence for its truth is strong, stronger than for its falsity. When we say that Mr. P, a person, is credible, we do not mean that he is "true" in the sense that a proposition is true. We mean that Mr. P as a person—that system of intentions, motives, and other "entities"—is authentic, sincere, free from self-serving intentions, as well as being in a position to certify P on epistemological noetic grounds. As indicated previously, the introduction of the notion of credibility is tantamount to reintroducing the moral dimensions into cognition, for morality has to do with intentions, principles, and motives; whereas science does its best to wash these considerations out of its considerations. Is it going too far to suggest that in all social "science" credibility is more central than truth?

Is not this the import of such notions as *Verstehen* and Søren Kierkegaard's argument that subjectivity is the truth? And is not this the point of Vico's distinction between data that are given to human knowers and therefore in some degree alien and unknowable and data that man creates and to which he is therefore privy? Insofar as the social sciences scrutinize the ways of human beings in their collective life, persons are their data. But they are not wholly public data. They cannot be wholly externalized into propositions that then can be assessed for their empirical truth. The difference between these kinds of data is illustrated by the different ways in which statistical generalizations are viewed by social science and by the individuals who constitute the sample upon which the statistics are based.

We have impressive statistics on the safety of air travel. The figures show without much doubt that air travel in commercial aircraft is safer than almost any other form of transportation and certainly far less dangerous than ordinary automobile travel. But whenever there is an air disaster in which hundreds of passengers lose their lives, the statistics are of small comfort either to the victims or their families. To them, *who* died is the only relevant fact; to the statistics, and we may add, to social science, *who* is of no import whatever.

Clearly, travel by air is a reasonable choice because of the odds against accidents. Confidence is impaired when reports about near-misses and human errors on the part of air personnel are published, even though they have not as yet affected the statistics. Such reports lower the credibility of the airplane industry despite the good statistics. To sum it up, existentially, the anguished or exalted cry "why me?" is of the utmost relevance; statistically, it is always beside the point.

With the help of a hyphen, one can call the separation of truth claims of propositions from their existential contexts "de-valuation" or "de-moralization." It is this separation that creates the credibility gap, especially when the boundaries are erected by technical language and elaborate procedures known only to the members of the profession or to some academic guild or to some department of officialdom. Yet these are our sources of knowledge and expert counsel in matters affecting individual and public welfare. Hence, it is important to examine more closely how these credibility questions arise in our dealings with academics and professions.

REFERENCES

1. Dialogue with John Searle in Bryan Magee, *Men of Ideas* (New York: Viking Press, 1978), pp. 192–93.

2. In the history of Harvard's attempts to make the study of public policy and service part of the university's professional offerings, the relation between professionalism, specialization, and procedural complexity can be discerned, although President Bok made the case for them on the grounds that the federal government suffered from having too many specialists who lacked general skills in administration and policy analysis. The development of these studies, both at Harvard and other institutions, indicates, I believe, that like other professional fields subjected to the academic scalpel, policy studies are now characterized by esoteric language, organizational theory, decision-making games, and procedural flow charts. Leonard and Mark Silk, "Be Serviceable," *Harvard Magazine* 83 (1980): 42–49.

3. Paul Johnson, *Enemies of Society* (New York: Atheneum, 1977), p. 206.

4. Stephen J. Noren, "Anomalous Monism, Events, and the 'Mental,'" *Philosophy and Phenomenological Research* 40 (1979): 72–73.

5

The Credibility of Professors and Professionals

If truth should reign anywhere, it is in the academy. The academic establishment professes to devote itself to the discovery, testing, and disseminating of knowledge, the truth—and to a large extent it does just that. Cardinal Newman in his *Idea of a University* gave it the duty of protecting all knowledge and science. The university catalogue reports in detail where, how, and by whom these activities are carried on. The lower schools induct pupils into this knowledge by studying selections from the arts and sciences.

The whole enterprise is legitimated by the methods of scholarship. The academic guilds (disciplines) guarantee the method and its proper application. What the guild certifies as warranted assertion is presumably free from personal, idiosyncratic, and nontheoretical interests. Unswerving loyalty to this ideal is implied in the contract between the community and the academic world. Is it then seemly to ask about the credibility of the legitimating authority itself?

One would like to respond with a quick and resounding no. Surely academics have kept the faith. But what if some "respectable" and "distinguished" men of science report as truth theories that justified the extermination of Jews in Germany? What about using "scientific" findings to legitimate other versions of racism?[1] We are told, for example, that the Reverend Sun Myung Moon's Unification Church financed superlevel international conferences of academics on a lavish scale. Multi-thousand-dollar honoraria were said to be offered to more than 400 distinguished academics. More accepted than refused.[2] Now suppose Academic A reads a learned paper at one of these conferences. Does the fact that he accepted a very generous honorarium affect the truth of his paper? Under what conditions might Professor A convince us that his findings are not contaminated by nonscientific factors? Aside from professional competence, which we have to take on our faith in his guild, that A does not stand to gain financially or politically would enhance his credibility; it would be enhanced even more if the paper threatened undesirable consequences for himself and for the Reverend Moon. It is interesting to note that for an academic to raise the question of Professor A's credibility lays him open to charges of hypocrisy or envy. Hypocrisy if he has benefited from similar invitations; envy if he has not. To establish credibility as a critic one would have had to be invited to the luxurious conference, offered a generous honorarium, and had refused the invitation or the honorarium or both. This dilemma is very effective in silencing criticism of academics by other academics.[3]

THE PROFESSORS

The credibility of academics has become a problem in proportion as they have become involved in nonacademic pursuits: consultants to government and industry or employees of these establishments. It was almost inevitable that the marketplace criteria of success should rub off on the academic ones. Although academics have been used by government since World War I, the rate was dramatically accelerated during the 1960s. When called to Washington, they were given a taste of and readily acquired a taste for good living and power. Professors, especially prestigious ones, are supposed to influence government by their superior knowledge; however, there is some reason to suspect that academics investigate what government wants to know. An example is the synchrony between Washington and academic attitudes toward defense, security, and arms policy. At this writing, more academics are becoming concerned with and therefore studying the decline in American power.[4]

Furthermore, salaries not only rose higher than academics were wont to expect, but became symbols of academic quality. Finally, the grant system provided a clear, if not always appropriate, yardstick of academic accomplishment. The economic incentive, which traditionally the professoriat renounced or repressed, now had a legitimate place in the marketplace of ideas. Today, any attempt by the professoriat to deny this motive or the yardstick invites, alas, a challenge to their credibility. The pervasiveness of grantsmanship is illustrated in the following: "In Minneapolis students participating in a three-high school integration program decide what the program needs to make it work and then write a proposal for federal funds to get started."[5]

A past president of the American Psychological Association wrote in a special issue of the association's newspaper that "psychology has joined the regressive movement toward self-interest and status." We are in danger, Dr. Albee said, "of becoming like the American Medical Association and other fat-cat guilds—self-serving and manipulative."[6]

Daniel S. Greenberg, editor and publisher of *Science and Government Report*, writes in a syndicated column that no one knows how much scientific cheating is going on. The refereeing process is less rigorous than one might expect and replication of experiments is "relatively rare." For one thing, he observes, that "in today's scarcity economy, no research foundation wants to put much money into repeating old experiments."

In a report of the twenty-eighth All University Faculty Conference on applied and public service research in the University of California, one former director of the Assembly Office of Research described what he called the "subtle corruption" of the university research effort. He grounded the alleged corruption on three pillars: monetary self-interest, bureaucratic status, and an extreme interpretation of academic freedom.[7] "Congress . . . permitted 'research' to become the vehicle for pouring federal assistance into the university system. And, not surprisingly, research, with its own *mores*, values, and rewards, tended to overwhelm the educational function of many universities."[8]

Yet when all the skepticism about the moral purity of the academics is taken into account, it does not really amount to much. While a few professors have power by virtue of their relationships with government or industry, most academics do not. On the contrary, part of the mystique of the professoriat is that it need not be taken seriously in the "real" world outside the classroom or the library. In place of influence, academics gain the freedom to play with ideas in the presence of their students and colleagues. This is their unique function in the social order, for in playing with ideas *ad libitum*, some ideas emerge that are of use outside the academy. China, trying to reverse this order of things, found that putting professors to work part-time in the fields and factories did not utilize their playful talents. For these reasons the public must learn to tolerate some side effects of some academic freedom from social responsibility.

An example of a problem that has great social import is that of the objectivity of standards as to what is true, real, and valuable. It is not surprising, therefore, that it has been a perennial question of great interest to professional philosophers, that is, academic philosophers. The literature on the topic is vast, but much of it is more a display of intellectual play than an attempt to improve society. Books rising to ever higher levels of abstraction and subtlety are written on the problem. Yet these exercises in language and logic rarely affect those who make ethical judgments or work in science laboratories. Scientists do not wait for philosophers to settle this issue, and philosophers are not held to any consequences of their language games. Yet we do not rush to abolish philosophy departments, nor should we, if we understand that the culture is apt to grow at its extremities, in its play with possible variations. The issues on which a culture disagrees are the interesting issues, as William James once observed. Alfred N. Whitehead warned ". . . the race which does not value trained intelligence is doomed. . . ." Playing with ideas is one way of training intelligence.

A more direct removal of the academy from social relevance is the specialism of scholarship. Academic specialism, the mark of high-level scholarship, has always suffered from a somewhat derisive, if not hostile, press. It has been chided for knowing more and more about less and less, for pedantry and logic chopping. The physical sciences are spared this contumely because of their ability to come up with useful applications in agriculture, medicine, or industry; but not all academic specialties can escape the amused bewilderment of the layman. In the humanities and the arts, the more minute the scholarship, the lower the credibility. In neither the sciences nor the humanities does the citizen comprehend the necessity for highly technical and esoteric terminology, but he will tolerate them if they produce results he can understand. Some scholarship in some of the academic disciplines he is asked to accept and support on no grounds that he can discern. There are several reasons for this.

For one thing, a great number of scholarly researches are Ph.D. theses written to demonstrate that the skills of the trade in a particular discipline have been mastered. Inasmuch as many of these learned exercises are never read by anyone, including the writer, after the doctoral examination, the citizen may be pardoned for not appreciating their intrinsic worth.

For another, much of the erudition in the academic world is the result of the high place research holds in the academic hierarchy. Subtlety breeds more subtlety. Hairs are split again and again; myths are exploded and invented. It must be remembered that many professors spend their lives seeking tenure and training Ph.D.'s who in turn will do research in order to get tenure and be referred to as "noted" scholars.

As an example, Gore Vidal, reviewing *Shikasta* by Doris Lessing, commented : "Currently, there are two kinds of serious novel. The first deals with the Human Condition (often confused, in Manhattan, with marriage) while the second is a word-structure that deals only with itself . . . . The word-structure novel is intended to be taught, rather like a gnostic text whose secrets may only be revealed by tenured adepts in sunless campus chapels."[9]

As another example, a book called *Alexander the Great and the Logistics of the Macedonian Army* by Donald W. Engels (Berkeley, Calif.: University of California Press, 1979),[10] throws light on the problems of supply encountered by Alexander's armies and other campaigns of the time. An army having devastated the supply of a countryside could not return by the same route. This is an important insight, but it is arrived at by minute and laborious discussion of statistics about the weight of supplies a camel could carry. To the lay reader camel loads may be of no significance in themselves. Or if he does happen to be interested in camels, the logistics of the Macedonian army may be a distraction. What to the academic is an ingenious use of data and statistics for the establishment of a historical point, to the lay reader may be no more than superfluous erudition.

The notorious Golden Fleece Awards by Senator Proxmire make fun of research the relevance of which to any human concern he cannot discern. Gross antiacademic philistinism aside, there may be a reason for the impatience with some forms of specialism. In some, the possible relevance of the experiment to wider uses is so unfamiliar that it is easy to infer that there is no relevance. Some of the recently reported experiments in DNA research with naked mice might baffle the layman, but if the experiment is done in a reputable university, he will take the relevance on faith. On the contrary, the point of a survey of the fast-food preferences of subway riders may be baffling indeed. Golden Fleeces are rarely awarded to technical research in the sciences, however unfamiliar the terminology. The opacity of the scientific technical language is a protective covering insulating them from ridicule. Social sciences projects are doubly vulnerable to the Golden Fleece hunt. If they are stated in ordinary language, the layman feels free to pass judgment on their social importance. If highly abstract language is used, for example, "interorganizational feedback" or "interpersonal affective relativity" to describe the project, the research is charged with needless obscurity and pretentiousness.

Much of the new history writing relies on data from marriage registers, census lists, tax lists, directories, and the like. From these, a theory about the economic status of slaves in the middle of the nineteenth century or the status of women in various times and countries is constructed. In contrast to such familiar entities, research into mesons, lasers, and chemicals with long names uses data that are themselves part of a highly abstract and related set of concepts. The weights of camel loads just do not compare with the weights of the elements in the atomic tables with respect to intellectual respectability. A project that had no further identification and explanation than an "Inquiry into Camel Loads during the Macedonian Conquests" is far more likely to get the Golden Fleece than one titled "The Influence of Weight Stress on Desert Ruminants."

In the American multipurpose university, the formal study of the several sciences and theoretical and applied research are located on the same campus. So are the professional schools of law, medicine, architecture, and engineering, to name a few. They are staffed by personnel who hold, for the most part, standard academic ranks, the very same as designate faculty in the liberal arts. The difference in power and prestige between the scientific-professional professoriat and those in the liberal studies is great and marked. To the former are attributed powers not unlike those that in ancient days belonged to alchemists and ecclesiastical officials. The latter have nothing remotely comparable to such reasons for reverence.

WHAT IS ACADEMIC "QUALITY?"

Professors of the humanities have little hope of making their case by social usefulness or increased market value. Undergraduates know this, as recent declines in enrolments give ample witness. It is doubtful that liberal education can maintain its place in the university, although general studies required by this or that preprofessional curriculum may survive. Even excellence in teaching cannot do much for the "prestige" of the humanities professor because teaching is not the key to the prestige of the scientists.

What, then, can serve as a yardstick of quality for the entire faculty? Although it is not easy to identify this quality, a fair approximation is intellectual caliber or theoretical competence. And the key word for intellectual caliber is *research*. If it can be shown that a professor does or has to do research, then his intellectual caliber is certified, no matter in which discipline it is done. A quality institution, therefore, is one that rewards research by recruiting staff that will do research, who will attract students who will also do research. If such faculties can snare grants for the research, the claim to prestige is established beyond doubt. Various self-appointed rating bodies make "research" the key criterion, and the professors whose opinions are the data for the ratings are themselves researchers.

Legislatures and boards of trustees are confronted annually with pleas for more money to maintain the "quality" of the institution. Without these extra funds, it is argued, star research professors will not come to the university and may be lured away to more lucrative posts. Understandably, some legislators and trustees are puzzled by these pleas. They understand that price is the measure of quality in the marketplace of commodities, but is it also the measure in the marketplace of ideas? Yes, the university administration affirms, pointing to the market value of the technological benefits derived from scientific research. But what is the market value of humanities or classics or literature professors? Here the administrator has to shift gears. "Quality," he suggests, means the caliber of mind required for advanced research and scholarship, and on this yardstick professors of history can be compared with professors of physics or chemistry. To be sure, their market values are not equal; nevertheless, a spirited bidding goes on for "top" history and literature scholars, and the reputation of a department demands the presence of such stars to attract other stars and star graduate students. Few university presidents, one may surmise, really convince the legislators and hard-headed trustees of the value of intellectual "quality" on purely intellectual grounds.

Their skepticism is not confined to the simultaneous assertion that (1) scholarly quality is not a commodity and therefore does not have an exchange value on the market and (2) that professorial salaries should reflect scholarly merit. The oddity does not end there. Academic merit, although presumably not measurable on a money scale, is judged by the number and size of research or study grants snagged and by the size of consultation fees received. It is not at all unusual for a professor to list absences from the university on "professional" assignments, usually for an honorarium, as evidence for a claim to a raise in salary. The ability to make money outside the university is coming to be good reason for salary increases inside the university. This is accepted as valid in corporate management; that it is being recognized as valid in the academic world tells us a good deal about the declining credibility of the academic establishment.

In the end it is the market that determines the salary. Thus medical school faculty and those in law and business schools command higher salaries than the professoriat in departments that are not feeders of personnel into lucrative occupations. These professors, moreover, can go into private practice if it becomes more lucrative to do so. In universities where research is valued above teaching and service—and a "good" university is defined as one that does—a research appointment is highly prized, not only because it releases the appointee from the chores of teaching, but also because the research counts more for rank and pay awards. Research appointees have a built-in advantage over colleagues who cannot escape from teaching and service on committees. Collective bargaining clears up many of these ambiguities about "quality".

Yet all these explanations somehow fail to change the attitude of the citizen toward the academic establishment, and perhaps of most legislators and members of boards of trustees. Perhaps the citizen has not fully abandoned loyalty to the traditional mystique of the university. The play of ideas, the search for truth, the nurture of young minds, transmission of the culture at its best—these functions were the *raison d'être* of the academy. Such a lofty function the citizen realizes is not left to the marketplace. The university or college, like other institutions, selectively assembles colleagues and students who develop a loyalty to the place, to each other, and to their special mission.

In this country during the 1960s the loyalty of the professor shifted from his institution to his colleagues in the discipline, wherever they might be. The "good" university was where one did what was "interesting" and promoted standing in one's guild. "Bright" people doing "interesting things" became the accepted criterion of university quality. "Interesting things" can be done by reading in the university library, but it is more likely that "interesting" things require travel to Tahiti, Hawaii, England, or the south of France, or at the least in the library of some other university. There is such a thing as academic glamour, and happily glamour also confers status. The traveling scholar is a rung or two above the run-of-the-mill stay at home.

It is of course true that circumstances the academic world did not invent account for the dependence of the university and scholars on federal and foundation grants. Nor has the university become a commodities trading post. Yet once academic quality acquires a price tag, the problem of credibility comes with it. It is difficult not to look at a price tag. Credibility is hard to maintain when a university president bemoans shrinking budgets and issues calls for austerity from an office that would do credit to an official of General Motors. There may be good reasons for an institution with a $400 million budget not to fill an assistant professor vacancy because it can no longer "afford" the $15,000 salary, but it does strain the institution's credibility.

The importance of maintaining the credibility of the academic establishment cannot be overestimated. For knowledge to be useful in the marketplace or elsewhere, some people have to pursue it for its own sake, and the public must never lose faith that the pursuit is not compromised by a price tag.

THE PROFESSIONALS

The public, perversely, persists in taking the rhetoric of the learned professions seriously, namely, that their primary loyalty is to the client and the public good. They do not like to treat the services of physicians, lawyers, clergymen, and teachers as market commodities. Sensible persons who would not dream of asking business or tradespeople to give their services gratis to the needy rather expect professionals to do so. One grim result of demystifying this mystique is the spate of malpractice suits against professionals. The suits carry price tags; they monetize morality.

Syndicated columnists and other pundits have commented at length on the effects of specialism in the professions and the sacrifice of social responsibility to monetary advantage. The scientists invent drugs that threaten the health of unwitting patients; pesticides that endanger community health. Architects design developments that create social ghettos and life in high rise edifices are subject to the risk of both crime and fire. The fortunes amassed by lawyers and physicians are reported gleefully in the media, and this in the face of increases in costs to those who can least afford to pay for them. The theme is the same; the variations virtually endless. The creation of the atomic bomb was the crowning evidence that between the power of science and its moral responsibility yawned a frightening, perhaps an unbridgeable, chasm. These sentiments, it is safe to say, express the citizen's perception of professional integrity. And while knowledge as such does not hold so exalted a place in professional schools as it does with scholars in the disciplines, the trust the layperson places in the professional's advice is far greater than that bestowed on the scholar. Professionals, especially the learned professionals, serve their clienteles in crisis situations: illness, threat of incarceration, imminent death, and so forth. They are the secular intercessionaries for the layperson who does not have the arcane knowledge needed in the crisis. As more and more of the services are professionalized, that is, as they become based in technical disciplines, they too join what someone has called the "high-minded callings."

Because of the special knowledge, the crisis character of the client's need, or both, society implicitly forms a special pact with the professions. In return for prestige and trust, the professional will render the service whenever needed. The money return is not the price of a commodity, but rather a gratuity, a thanks offering of the client. Understandably, poor clients give smaller gratuities than rich ones. Because the client has no way of verifying for himself the prescriptions of the professional, he depends almost entirely on trust in his competence and integrity. Hence the relationship between client and professional is highly moralized, a relationship that professionals jeopardize as their services are monetized by a fee system and de-moralized by specialization.

How society should reward its learned professionals was a problem raised by Plato in the *Republic*, when he proscribed private families and fortunes for the Guardians. The church has faced this difficulty through the ages and so has the academy. If not the marketplace, then what should determine professional stipends? Living in monasteries and convents at the expense of the Order and at a level determined by the Order? Are they to be "patronized" by princes as artists have been? Ideally, their monetary stipends should enable them to live in the manner required by their office or profession. But how is one to determine this? If professors, lawyers, and physicians are to educate their children properly and keep up their health and competence, and if they are to be reasonably free of money problems, then the stipend might be large indeed. The present fee system of recompense is not adequate either. Physicians and professors are not distributed equally in town and city; not all who need their services have equal access to them.

And yet, and yet . . . the public even in its most grateful mood toward their intercessionaries cannot bring themselves to believe that they require huge incomes, pleasure palaces, and life styles that compete with that of entertainment celebrities and industrial tycoons. Unreasonable? Perhaps. Irrational? Possibly. Incredible? Perhaps not.

When, however, all the feet of clay are exposed it is difficult to believe that the damage to the credibility of the professions can be attributed wholly to money. More important is the concern that the law, medicine, and other learned callings are no longer primarily dedicated to the public good. It is the suspicion that the professions are more concerned with the procedures and rules of their calling than with their consequences on other value domains. Procedural correctness is still regarded as an adequate defense against charges of malpractice. Regardless of the consequences to the client or the community, professional morality stops with legitimated procedures. Departing from the approved procedures, even when they produce beneficial results, makes the guild apprehensive.

THE LAW

Perhaps the most familiar example of de-moralization by procedures is that of the law. The public grits its teeth and bears it with a shake of the head as putatively the lesser of many other possible evils, but it never quite accepts its rightness. To the citizen, there is a difference between complicated civil and criminal court actions involving large corporations, celebrities, and other powerful interests and those that he hears about in the local or county courts. The former, the citizen will agree, has no clear-cut "right" and "wrong" that is obvious to common sense. Only an orderly and formal court procedure will suffice to manage such complexity. The citizen may suspect the influence of money and politics in such cases, but it remains a vague suspicion based on hunches and gossip.

The case is quite different when a janitor confesses to the rape of a schoolteacher in a local school and gets off with a short sentence in jail because of "technicalities." Technicalities are defended by citing instances in which lynching mobs in their lust for revenge hanged the wrong man —as it later turned out—and it is better to let many guilty men escape rather than punish one innocent one. However, even the most complicated procedures cannot guarantee that an innocent person will not be found guilty. Reducing the number of convictions may reduce the number of innocent victims, assuming that the accused are evenly divided between the innocent and the guilty, but the principle can be carried to absurdity, and when it is, the whole system loses credibility.

From time to time, victims of a crime are outraged by the adroit legalistic use of defendant rights to evade punishment altogether or a punishment commensurate with the harm inflicted on them. Such outrage is countered by the doctrine that the trial is between the accused and the state. The victim, it has been said, is the occasion and vehicle of the drama and not a principal actor. Hence the injuries suffered by the victim and the recompense for them are not the concern of the system of criminal justice.

Divorcing fairness to the accused by enforcing constitutional rights from fairness to the victim by recompense for injury may have good logical grounds, but it detracts from the credibility of the legal profession. This happens not only because it is *unreasonable* to demand that the victim substitute putative public benefits for palpable and indubitable injury but also because it is hard for him to believe that lawyers and judges would be able to do so if they were the victims. The use of the logically defensible distinction is regarded as an attempt to evade a moral situation —itself a species of immorality.

The problem of truth versus credibility is daily fare in the practice of the law. Whenever litigants appear in court, they make divergent claims based on the nature of some event—a contract, an accident, a crime of one sort or another. The immediate task for the judge and jury is to determine what did *in fact* happen and *how* it happened. And even when the two parties agree that there was in fact a collision between their respective vehicles at such and such a place and at such a time, they may not agree as to what or who caused the collision.

Determining what and how an event occurred presents a truth problem inasmuch as some of the details cannot be ascertained at all, especially if accounts of witnesses differ. The real story is usually not in the best interests of *both* parties. Hence the elaborate system of rules by which the court determines not what really happened but rather which side had the better of the debate carried on by opposing counsel according to the rules of evidence.[11] The quest for truth is given up in favor of a formal debate on credibility. This has been called formal truth as distinguished from substantive truth.

And yet, Max Radin notes, despite formalization, and judging by rules and precedents or in accordance with statutes, judges want their decisions to be just as well as correct. They want this despite the elusiveness of the concept in philosophy and in law. But why? Aside, that is, from satisfying the allegedly innate sentiment of justice? Presumably because they seek credibility for themselves as judges over and beyond formal correctness, which conceivably a machinelike computer-judge could render better than a human one. This credibility does not affect the content of the judgment as much as it does the judgment by the public of the judge as a person. "Judges," says Radin, "make law. Justice makes judges." He also notes: "And since our community is far too heterogeneous to permit the comfortable assumption that our fund of common characteristics will secure an extensive common sentiment of justice, we are not well advised if we make conformity to our sense of justice too prominent an element in our demand on the judge . . . . But nothing will tempt us to forego it completely."[12]

Toward the end of its 1979–80 term the Supreme Court settled cases involving abortion, freedom of the press, working safety, and racial quotas. These cases were the occasions for an impressive display of the attempts of the legal apparatus to cope with social, political, and moral issues. The votes were 5 to 4, 7 to 1, 5 to 4, and 6 to 3. The four cases produced no fewer than 212 concurring and dissenting opinions, filling 345 pages. The splintering of the Court decisions reflects the complexity of the cases. But it is a complexity of heterogeneous complexes. The ideologies of the justices differ; the laws and legal precedents vary, and above all judgments as to relevance vary.

To the citizenry in this country the U.S. Supreme Court is a relief, for a while at least, from the merry-go-round of legalistic procedures as the participants shuffle and circle through indictments, trials, appeals, injunctions, judgments, stays, and hearings.[13] Moreover, the credibility of the Court is about as high as that of any government institution can be. The ordinary temptations to serve selfish interests have been removed by high salaries, life tenure, and great prestige. Nevertheless, the justices were chosen by politicians for reasons that were not free of politics. And what is even more important, the justices not only have their ideology but they are almost expected to allow their opinions to reflect them.

To the citizen, the facing of moral issues by the Court is worth some loss of technical objectivity. Exposure of ideological and other nonlegalistic factors in the judgment of the Justices (for example, *The Common Brethren* by Robert Woodward and Scott Armstrong) does not outrage the electorate as much as might be expected. Credibility depends more on frankness and sincerity than on formal correctness. A Court decision that in the name of legal correctness violates the moral sense of justice of the public harms the credibility of the Court far more than dissent on honestly held ideological grounds. It would seem as if the public trusts the Supreme Court, not because it is above moral considerations, but because it does take them into account.

Nor does the public become cynical about the Supreme Court because from time to time it changes its emphases. It does not expect the justices to achieve the perfect intuition of perfect and immutable justice. It does expect honesty, sincerity, and strong evidence that as persons the justices do not stand to profit personally from their decisions. It is not the absence of interest that determines their credibility but the lack of a conflict of interest.

An American Bar Association commission report on Rules of Professional Conduct cites occasions when the lawyer should blow the whistle on a client's prospective criminal acts, or when he intends to injure other persons or mislead a judge or jury. But according to one journalist, the report is in for some rough sledding. That the study was undertaken at all in the face of the chorus of opposition from members of the bar signifies the recognition that the public's confidence in the legal profession's ability to police itself is low, so low that there is some fear that government may step in and impose rules on it.[14]

There is no need to examine all the professions in detail. All could furnish examples of specialism accelerating the general shift from substance to procedure. They could also serve as examples of the demoralization that specialism almost necessitates. For to specialize is to exclude as many troublesome considerations as possible from a self-limited domain. It carves an area of activity out of the life context and refuses to restore the connections to other domains. If morality means the obligation to be concerned with consequences, especially human consequences, then such arbitrary self-limitation borders on the amoral and even on the immoral.

It is therefore not surprising that specialism engenders loss of credibility and raises questions of the professional's motivation. And although the client may out of ignorance be in a better moral state, there is no lack of evidence that, given an opportunity, some clients will in collusion with a professional conspire to defraud the government, insurance companies, and hospitals. This forces us to temper the moral indignation that laypersons sometimes express at the nonprofessional behavior of professionals. It is also why "moralism" has such a bad name; it is too often a close relative of hypocrisy.

REFERENCES

1. Cf. Michael Billig, *Psychology, Racism, & Facism* (Birmingham, England: A.F. & R. Publications, 1979).

2. Irving L. Horowitz, ed., *Science, Sin, and Scholarship: The Politics of Reverend Moon and the Unification Church* (Cambridge, Mass.: MIT Press, 1979).

3. See articles on hypocrisy, illusion, and evasion in *Daedalus* 108, no. 3 (Summer 1979).

4 Richard Burt, "A New Fashion of Toughness Among the Eggheads of War," *New York Times*, 13 July 1980, p. 22E.

5. *American Education* 15, no. 8 (October 1979): 1.

6. As reported by Dava Sobel, *New York Times*, 7 September 1980.

7. Of course, universities have never been wholly free from political and financial influences, as the history of Paris and Oxford shows.

8. Daniel Greenberg, *The Politics of Pure Science*, quoted in Colin Norman, *Knowledge and Power: The Global Research and Development Budget* (Washington. D.C.: Worldwatch Institute, July 1979), p. 24

9. *New York Review of Books* 26 (20 December 1979): 3.

10. *See* E. Badian's review, *ibid*, pp. 54 ff.

11. At times the court invokes rituals to ensure that the truth will be demanded; for example, taking on oath, or undergoing ordeals. Max Radin, "The Permanent Problems of the Law," in *Jurisprudence in Action: An Anthology of Legal Essays* (New York: Baker Voorhis, 1953), pp. 415–46.

12. *Ibid.*, pp. 422 and 426.

13. The Case of the Clerical Collar is another example of how procedures come to have a life of their own and after a while displace the substantive issues they are supposed to manage. According to The *New York Times*, 13 July 1980, in 1974 a man of the cloth serving as a lawyer in a jury trial was forbidden by the court to wear his collar, a decision reversed by a state supreme court justice. A year later this reversal was reversed, and this was upheld. In 1976 the U.S. Supreme Court refused to review the case. In 1979 another judge in the state supreme court ruled in favor of the cleric and his collar. The appellate court reversed this judgment. In 1980 an appeal to the federal district court kept the case alive.

14. Linda Greenhouse, "The Lawyers Struggle to Uphold Their Own Ethics," *New York Times*, 10 February 1980, p. 10E.

6

Economics, Truth, and Credibility

No sphere of citizen conduct is more ubiquitous and more insistent than the economic one. No value domain is without its economic conditions. Indeed, as will be noted from time to time, we are approaching the time when a money price is the accepted measure of all values. In sports, for example, a tennis tournament is reported as the "$150,000 tournament," and the name of a football star is almost never mentioned without note of his salary. The importance of evangelism programs on television is measured by the amounts of money they cost and yield. Perhaps for the first time in history we can compare unambiguously the worth of a Van Gogh painting, a popular entertainer, and a palimony settlement. Money not only talks but talks in a *lingua franca* that needs no gloss.[1]

It might be expected, therefore, that knowledge on which to make economic decisions rationally should have reached a high level of reliability. And it should be reasonable to expect that the custodians and purveyors of this knowledge should be the economists, and indeed they seem to be. Their pronouncements are taken seriously by government, industry, and the general public. Wassily Leontief, a Nobel Prize winner, commented in his presidential address to the 83rd meeting of the American Economic Association (20 December 1970), that "economics today rides the crest of intellectual responsibility and popular acclaim."

Economics has reached a high level of sophistication and abstraction, but it is no secret that economists cannot agree on an explanation of inflation, recession, growth, lack of growth, and other signs of economic malaise. Says Edward Cowan, "It is all a reminder that despite the sophisticated theories of Keynesian fiscal policy and Friedmanite monetary policy, those who practice political economy—economists as well as politicians—have yet to show that they can flatten the business cycle."[2] Conservative economists blame inflation on budget deficits and urge less government regulation of private enterprise. Liberals want tax incentives to encourage price-wage restraints. Perhaps, as Leontief noted, it is because "as an academic science, economics . . . has been concerned with reasoning, neglectful of information."[3]

Three economic experts, asked to predict the growth in the gross national product in 1981, in September of 1980 came up with highly reasoned forecasts of 3.4 percent, −1.3 percent, and −3 percent. The three graphs for the quarters of the coming year had little resemblance to one another. Businessmen, let alone the plain citizen, despair of solid economic predictions for making their plans.

Whatever rationality the citizen would like to exhibit in his economic decisions is frustrated by the apparent inability of economic scholarship to explain and predict the vagaries of the market, which, according to Adam Smith, should be controlling itself by the immutable laws of supply and demand. That economists or economic statisticians nevertheless are fully employed is due, one may suppose, to a need for economic data, to tell us what *has* happened to the price index, balance of payments, price of gold, interest rates, and the like. That these data do not yield uniform generalizations and reliable predictions is a puzzling anomaly to the public.

No doubt some economists are also puzzled by this anomaly. Perhaps the apparatus of quantification and gathering of "hard" data gives the impression that economics is closer to a natural science than it really is. The elaborate apparatus of financial reporting is useful to the expert and specialist. News of mergers, especially prospective ones, is important to the financial world, and so are the trends on the stock and bond markets. Wall Street is carpeted from wall to wall with analysts and services that extrapolate trends of all sorts into predictions about how the market will behave—if it behaves as it has before. There are contrarians who design their investment strategy in opposition to the prevailing view of the majority of the analysts.

The nonspecialist citizen finds most of this news and speculation unintelligible. To find in the masses of figures and reports grounds for expecting inflation to persist or desist, or whether mortgage rates will go up or down, or whether the government's policy on taxes is to be supported or resisted—these are inferences the citizen cannot draw on logical grounds. For one thing, the language of economics, especially that of finance, is too technical for the nonspecialist.[4] Nor does the citizen understand the complexity of the situations that economic theory is trying to capture in a conceptual framework. Daily life confirms the complexity, and the financial section of any metropolitan newspaper compounds it. Of all sections in the paper, this one baffles the general reader the most. And yet, although the terminology of the futures commodity market is esoteric and technical, such terms as "supply" and "demand" are so close to ordinary language as to be vulnerable to inexactness.

Anyone who regards this observation as extreme, exaggerated, or just inaccurate should consult a full-page discussion of our economic situation in the *New York Times*, 13 July 1980, p. E3. The participants were economists Robert Lekachman; Ray Marshall, Secretary of Labor; and Herbert Stein, chairman of the Council of Economic Advisors in the Nixon and Ford administrations. The impenetrability of the "expert" briefing, which is far from being unrepresentative, may help to explain the following statistics: In a Gallup poll taken 27–29 June 1979, 11 percent "didn't know" whether they preferred "increased government spending," "tax cuts," or "neither" as a means of stimulating the economy. Twenty percent answered "don't know" whether a tax cut would increase, decrease, or have no effect on inflation.

ECONOMIC THEORIES

If there is one economic theory with which the lay citizenry is almost intuitively familiar, it is that of the free market. It hypothesizes that humans beings seeking to maximize their economic welfare will sell as dearly as they can and buy as cheaply as they can. The engine of the system is gratification of the desire for material goods; given this desire, production, consumption, distribution, investment, and labor will automatically adjust themselves so that each is achieving the maximum gain. An Invisible Hand manages the adjustment in an objective, impersonal, inexorable way, and the safest course is not to interfere with it. The state or the government should restrict its activities to keeping crooks and violent attacks on property down to a minimum.

At the other pole is the somewhat less familiar theory of an economic system in which production, distribution, and investment are controlled by the state; by a corporate state as in Mussolini's Italy or by the Communist party as in the Soviet Union. On Marxist theory, the state should wither away after the productive forces have achieved their full potential under the dictatorship of the proletariat. On the Marxian theory the economic system at any particular time marks the historic status of the struggle between social classes. At present in the West, capitalists are exploiting labor, and the latter are waiting patiently or impatiently for inevitable historic forces to overthrow capitalism in favor of the proletariat.

If these characterizations sound simplistic, they are nevertheless the way the citizen formulates them, and this is how the arguments and debates in the press on economic policy are interpreted. But naive as the citizenry may be, their experience tells them every day that government does interfere in a free enterprise system and that governments in totalitarian countries do not have complete control of their economic systems. Above all, they doubt that the free enterprise capitalistic system in this country or, better, the mixed economy of this country, is fair, just, and really efficient. Very few of the poor believe that they deserve to be poor, far fewer than the prosperous citizens who attribute success to their own ability and efforts.

Nor can citizens be persuaded that they all start the economic race at the same mark. The laws of inheritance see to it that they do not. Clearly, large corporations, "mom-and-pop" stores, and day laborers do not run the race on the same course. Neither does it escape the citizen that the economic race is not rerun anew each month or year or even every fifty years.[5] The strong and most able who win the first race can also fix the rules so that they and their offspring can more easily win subsequent races, generation after generation. Revolutionary reforms of society can be regarded as demands to start the race over again under new rules.

Very confusing to the layperson are the retorts of economic theorists to their critics. For example, when a free enterpriser is shown instance after instance in which the market does not determine prices or productivity, the answer is that the system has been tainted by government interference or by private monopoly, and therefore is no longer free. Conversely, when it is argued that state-controlled economies do not produce sufficient consumer goods or permit corruption and waste in their factories, the retort is that capitalistic influences on the psyche of the people remain and interfere with the system. As Sommers points out:

> In conventional equilibrium economics, the market is thus the supreme mechanism, free of all critical criteria, insulated by its own axioms from all criticism. Whatever it does is right, by virtue of its having done it, in much the same way that whatever nature does (for example, the creation of the snail darter) is right. . . .
>
> In the real world, of course, such absolute positions are rarely warranted. The outcomes produced by the free market, and the outcomes foregone by the free market, do not necessarily add up to a livable, survivable world by modern standards, much less the best of all possible worlds. . . .[6]

This quotation succinctly states the problem the free market theory poses for the citizen. First, how could such a theory be proved or even tested, if in the real world no example of it exists and perhaps could not exist? For the conditions demanded by the theory to exist, human beings would have to be almost exclusively dominated in virtually everything they do by material needs and wishes. Yet health, recreation, love, pride, patriotism, truth, justice, and beauty are from time to time desired and sought for their own sake as well as for material gain and occasionally in spite of economic loss. In the second place, in what sense can an economic system be free and yet be a "supreme mechanism, free of all critical criteria, insulated by its axioms from all criticisms?"

The loss of the theory's credibility is fueled by daily reports of chicanery, bribery, theft, corruption, and waste that presumably are not restrained by the Invisible Hand nor prevented by government. For example, in the *New York Times* for 30 September 1979 it was reported by Jeff Gerth that "an unpublicized civil trial in Canada has produced evidence that the Exxon Corporation, the world's largest oil company, systematically passed along artificially inflated prices to customers in Canada and elsewhere. . . . All this was conceded in testimony by Exxon officials or substantiated by Exxon documents entered into evidence." In the same issue another story described the proposed guidlines for business on the ban on bribery overseas. Whatever else the "free" market is, it is not free from the efforts of some corporations to subvert it.

And what is the citizen to infer about the free market from a report such as the following in the *New York Times*, 3 July 1980?

Landlords Charged in Arson for Profit

Fifteen men were indicted last week as members of an arson ring that, authorities said, made the buildings they burned pay off twice.

They collected fire insurance on the structures, then applied for government loans and subsidies to rehabilitate the properties.

District Attorneys Mario Merola of the Bronx and Eugene Gold of Brooklyn said the men were responsible for eight fires and had conspired to set 10 others that were thwarted over the last four years.

Most of the group are landlords or are involved in some other phase of the real estate industry. Two were described as "torches," the people who actually set the fires. Police said they were the largest arson-for-profit ring in the city.

These men are charged with breaking laws, but are laws that prevent energetic entrepreneurs from using their ingenuity to maximize their gains consistent with a free market theory? Or is the defect of those indicted that they did not accomplish their goals without breaking the law? If arsonists could find loopholes in the law, or if they could find lawyers who could find loopholes in the law forbidding people from setting fires, should not arsonists be applauded by free market enthusiasts? Unsubtle plain citizens may be, but they are embarrassed by those who try to persuade them that in the free market economy lies their salvation. The theory may be sound, but it lacks credibility.

The prospect of the citizenry being given information on which to ground economic decisions is not bright. Despite highly increased sophistication in gathering and processing economic data, the pure forms (the free enterprise market or the completely controlled market) assume nonexisting conditions so that their explanatory power does not increase with greater and more precise quantification.

There is in addition the strong possibility that the economist's predictions will become self-fulfilling or self-defeating prophecies. Thus predictions of higher inflation encourage activities that increase inflation; expectations of a recession tend to hasten it, thus contributing to the unfalsifiability of the theory. Of course it has never been possible to construe the Invisible Hand theory strictly, and it has been argued that "almost from start to finish, the classic era of capitalism had a religious and moral dimension, which in a sense contradicted its non-interventionist economic theory."[7]

A far more serious challenge to classical capitalistic economic theory is the Marxian thesis that capitalism is both a necessary stage in economic history and *necessarily* exploits the workers until their misery forces overthrow of the existing system of production. If true, this makes capitalism *necessarily* evil from a moral point of view because it has to inflict misery on masses of workers who, presumably, do not deserve it.

The appeal of communism is a moral one. It promises that when the means of production are finally socialized, the class struggle and exploitation will be over. Man will be reconciled with his work and fellow man. In the classless society the economic system will be just, taking from each according to ability and giving to each according to need. This moral claim has been the source of communism's appeal to the masses of have-nots who seem destined to outnumber the haves by the billions. The exclusion of moral considerations from economic theory and practice by many of the doctrinaire defenders of laissez-faire capitalism and political foes of government intervention in the economy is a dangerous as well as an hypocritical ploy. It is hypocritical because in practice capitalistic enterprises do not hesitate to accept government intervention and regulation when it is to their benefit; it is dangerous because what a democratic and free society will not or cannot provide in the way of social and economic justice, the perpetual majority of have-nots will try to achieve by revolution.

The historical and economic determinism so essential to Marxist theory does not comport well with its moral claims. Morality entails freedom to choose; some degree of indeterminism, even in economic activity, is implied by freedom. Just as God did not create man and leave it to Aristotle to make him rational, so it is unlikely that God left it to Marx to make him moral. And if man had a moral sense to begin with or very early in the game, then the history of economic development is not inevitably determined.

As to the inevitable blessings that will accrue from each one of us working in our own interest, Shlomo Maital says,

> Sometimes, people can achieve their ends not by working harder, saving more, or being more efficient, but at the expense of their neighbors. When beggar-my-neighbor psychology becomes widespread, only some form of constraints can help. Inflation now faces us all with just such a situation, one in which rational individuals acting legitimately in their own self-interest lead us all to collective ruin.[8]

These sentiments are reinforced by the ubiquitous network of pass-throughs justified as needed "if we are to stay in business" and "if we are to continue providing jobs." That the body politic is divided into those who can and those who cannot pass on the increased costs of inflation is perceived as "unfair." Efforts by government to "fair it up" are welcomed as "just" by those who cannot pass the increases on (e.g., those who live on fixed incomes, retirees) and as economic lunacy by the editors of the *Wall Street Journal* and the conservative members of both political parties.

The citizen's "noneconomic" sense of justice is further offended by reports of criminal elements preying on the economic system by both illegal and "legal" means, corruption in high and low places, and the shocking costs of trying to catch them, which are inevitably borne by the consumer. In sum, the public takes the Invisible Hand not to be the impersonal workings of universal law but a very palpable hand made invisible by force, fraud, chicanery, and chronic misrepresentation. So much so that Courtney C. Brown was moved to say: "Credibility will be restored only when business spokesmen are able to articulate a set of guiding principles that relate the conduct of business to a wide range of human aspirations, not just to material abundance alone."[9]

One might argue that economic theories are analogues to physical theories that describe and formalize what is found in the real world. If no moral or noneconomic factors are in the real world, then the theory need take no account of them. Whether an economic system is just or not would be irrelevant. In the real world an economic theory is regarded as normative as well as descriptive—economics at one time was regarded as a moral science—as prescriptive for maximizing not only economic but related human benefits, and in this sense it claims not only to be true but in some sense right as well. For the citizen, the question is not merely "How does the system work?" but "How can the system produce greater economic benefits?" So also we study military science not merely for an account of how battles were fought but for how they were won or lost.[10] In the real world, therefore, an economic theory that eschews moral considerations will be unbelievable in principle, and, given sufficient injustice and suffering, will become intolerable in practice. After all, economics at one time *was* regarded as a moral science.

THE HUMAN AND HUMANE DIMENSION

Why human beings should cease to display all their human characteristics in their economic behavior is hard for the lay citizenry to comprehend and renders economic theories that make this assumption incredible. Whether the theory postulates greed or class struggle as the motive of economic activity, the human participants do not shrink into economic men and women. The value network that constitutes the human agent envelopes all behavior, and although economic resources have an instrumental role in most of them, it is not solely for economic purposes that they are undertaken. The teeming populations of undeveloped nations are witness to the perdurance of noneconomic impulses.

The imagination operates in the economic sphere as in others. Imagination conjures up not only dreams of boundless material satisfactions but also clever schemes for exploiting one's fellow human beings. Economic activity for the sake of ego satisfaction, for power, or for prestige go beyond the supply-demand, producer-consumer schemata. The same imagination creates the notion of luck that will outwit the work-reward equation. All gambling, legal and otherwise, in Las Vegas or on Wall Street, depends on the anticipation and possibility of undeserved good fortune overriding the malign machinations of bad luck. It is the same imagination that can create the concepts of fairness, justice, and equity in the economic domain as in others.

Inevitably in a capitalist society—and perhaps in all societies—there will be congenital, or habitual, or innocent losers in the economic competition. It would not be a race if everybody won or lost all the time. That is why in judging societies at least three criteria need to be taken into account. One is the opportunity the society affords for talent and creativity to enlarge the volume of value possibility. Some societies rate higher than others on what might be called achievement potential. A second is justice, that system of government and law that keeps the conditions of the competition fair. In a complex and interdependent world, reward is not automatically adjusted to effort or merit, and it is naive as well as insensitive to assume that it does. Finally, there is a need for compassion. Some congenital and environmental factors produce losers, and a good society has a margin of compassion for them that overrides legal and even moral calculations of desert.[11]

The very complexity of the economic enterprise should give pause to complacent self-congratulation of the successful ones among us. We rely on the "system" with all its tangles and relations to sustain our own efforts. The whole communication system has to collaborate with every long-distance telephone call; hundreds of hands, eyes, and brains have to cooperate every time we ride a freeway or a modern aircraft, or buy a can of beans. The awareness of the tangle of interdependence, while it may annoy us by its complexity and ineptitude, should also make us conscious of our debt to it and to each other.

Our society ranks high on the criterion of achievement potential, and certainly is not on the lowest rung of justice and compassion. Yet the current wave of libertarianism under the guise of restoring freedom poses a real threat to both justice and compassion, for, as John Kenneth Galbraith has observed: "They are the friends of freedom, enemies of government. But none should be in doubt about the nature of their crusade. It is against the least fortunate of our citizens."[12] And as he points out, capitalism did not survive because of its hard-boiled adherence to individualism but because it had enough social concern "to soften its harsh edges—to minimize the suffering of those who fail in face of competition."

These considerations help explain why the public is moved to ask about the motives and ideology behind the espousal of an economic theory or policy. Whether the theory is "true" it cannot judge, but it can understand why the profit motive or the lust for power would lead some persons and institutions to preach the free market theory, and why professional and ideological motives might lead others to favor controlled economies. Clearly, to support a theory that does not favor one's own interests gives credibility to the sincerity of an individual or political party, but does it make the theory itself more credible? In at least two senses, it may. One is that there is less likelihood that the facts have been deliberately fudged or misinterpreted; the other is that advocating a theory that is not in one's interest strengthens the claim to objectivity.

A student who had majored in economics on reading this chapter felt compelled to say, "but..." after almost every paragraph. She was reflecting the fact that to almost every statement about the economy one can retort that there are other sides to the argument and other ways of analyzing it, and that something important is being left out. Unfortunately, the body politic, not having majored in economics, cannot make decisions on nicely balanced distinctions. For one thing, the citizen cannot make and often cannot understand the distinctions; for another, if he could, he might not make any decisions. For, as one noted economist has remarked:

> When economists wish to make their most modest claim to being scientists they compare themselves with meteorologists. The comparison is an apt one. When the morning weather forecast is for rain that day we are likely to take our umbrella with us when we leave the house. When, in September, we read a forecast that the coming winter will be unusually severe we do not rush out to buy extra heavy winter clothing. And when some expert writes that the earth's climate is warming up (or cooling down—there is disagreement here)

with dire foreboding for the next century we read it as we would science fiction and certainly do not alter our daily lives. I suspect that the futurist's [economic futurists that is] appeal is to that same desire in all of us to penetrate the impenetrable: their forecasts should be treated as we treat forecasts of long-range climate changes—or science fiction.[13]

The citizen, confused by theoretical subtleties and disagreements among the experts, adopts an economic theory or ideology not on the basis of its theoretical adequacy but rather on its congruence with a general value schema. The schema will include a conglomerate of beliefs about the value of work, the workplace, economic rewards, and other dimensions of the good life. Some of these beliefs and attitudes are rooted in dim prehistory; a primitive sense of balance is one of the roots. Perhaps the symmetry of the body, perhaps the balance between action and reaction in physical activity, perhaps the steady alternation between inhaling and exhaling in respiration gave birth to the notion of the rightness of balance. Balance is an instinctive norm, if such norms exist. From the sense of rightness as balance comes much of our notion of justice as the restoration of balance between injury and revenge, theft and restitution, crime and punishment.

Economic justice is no exception. Balance requires that rewards should be commensurate with effort, because effort is usually painful and the reward balances it. The more pain, the more recompense. Hard physical labor deserves more than sedentary work in a pleasant workplace. On this basis, the citizen, innocent of all theory, would agree that inequalities of reward are just if they match inequalities of contribution and sacrifice. He may appreciate the justice of rewarding risk taking and the postponement of gratification involved in saving. But he may not understand or appreciate the inequalities of reward that result from swindles, exploitation, and irresponsible speculation, and he may not be quite sure about the proper attitude to assume toward large money rewards for exercising a gift of nature or from exploiting the weaknesses of mankind.

As an example of this sense of fairness and balance is an inchoate awareness that inequality of economic benefits is not the same as inequality of sacrifice. One might agree with the traditional utilitarian theory of ethics and market economics that for the totality of goods and services to be maximized it may be necessary to allow some individuals much higher rewards than others. Managers, daring investors, inventors, and the like produce so much economic good for the body politic as a whole that it is only fair that their rewards be proportionately large. Thus the athletic star who draws huge crowds is entitled to an unusually high salary; everybody benefits from this inequality. Inasmuch as few individuals believe that they merit no more than anyone else taken at random, the consistent égalitarian, as far as wealth is concerned, is rare indeed.

Yet when it comes to sacrifice, the case, as the citizen senses, is not the same. For example, when the largest segment of the population is forced to bear the cost of an economic depression by a drastic reduction in living standards, while a minuscule segment narrows its scope of luxury a little, this inequality is hardly justifiable on the basis of the greatest good of the greatest number. Nor is the sacrifice of life by a conscripted soldier commensurable with the deprivations suffered by arms manufacturers and generals. Physical pain and bodily deprivation abrogate the relativity of sacrifice; such pain is not merely the loss of a benefit.

Great suffering by a few—volunteers for painful experiments with a new drug—conceivably could lessen the pain of a great number, but it is hard to imagine a situation in which maintaining the luxury of a few would diminish the suffering of the least advantaged members of the society, as Rawls stipulated in the justification for the inequality of benefits.[14] Where sacrifice is so extreme as to impair health, or even life itself, it would be a trifle odd to say that allowing a small number of owners and managers to maintain a high standard of living is justified if their taxes help support charity hospitals and free burial plots for masses of unemployed workers. As Winston Churchill once put it: "The inherent vice of capitalism is the unequal sharing of blessings; the inherent virtue of socialism is the equal sharing of miseries."

It is difficult for the citizen in reading economic literature to see life wholly through the lens of the economic incentive. Granted that physical needs are undeniable, the citizen believes that keeping the body alive and well is for the sake of experience what keeps the soul alive also. The common view is that money is instrumental to the achievement of other nonmonetary values, each with a unique intrinsic quality. The subjective quality of health, recreation, association, participation in civic affairs, the achievement of truth, the sense of duty and obligation, and the realization of the beautiful and the holy are distinctive, and their harmonization in some fashion is generally believed to be essential to the satisfaction with life as a whole.

Yet in our culture very few of these varied values escape the economic net. Entertainment, travel, study, and even association with friends and family entail money costs either as expenditures or as foregoing the use of time to earn income. One person's dollar spent on entertainment becomes income for those who provide the means for that entertainment. As a result, all experiences, regardless of intrinsic qualities, become anonymous droplets in the pool of goods and services, each translated into a money price. Hence the worth-cost equation is created, a useful construct for the hedonic calculus and for econometrics, but lacking credibility. Not a little of our difficulty with economic theory reflects the skepticism with which this equation is regarded.

VIRTUE AS AN ECONOMIC VALUE

In a capitalistic society, the citizen is persuaded that virtue has no economic value. The notion arises because the free market theory places so much stress on the primacy of economic incentives. This has a dual effect: one is to separate economic incentives from noneconomic ones and to give the latter short shrift (some would deny their existence). The other is to invite the inference that actions motivated by moral considerations are not likely to be profitable, and in any event irrelevant to economic decisions. The saying that virtue is its own reward suggests that it is its only reward. In other words, the desire to have one's action conform to some code of right or justice has to be suppressed if the economic costs and benefits are to be accurately assessed. Crime and greed are not restricted to capitalistic societies, but a capitalistic society increases the opportunities to satisfy that greed and the excuses for doing so. Unlike societies in which freebooting banditry is a privilege of the warrior class, our culture does not make raw greed for profit respectable unless very well laundered by a free market theory.

Our hypothetical citizen finds all this troubling and almost un-believable. Not being a "soul-less" corporation makes it difficult to regard the needs and interests of family and friends and the human needs of the community as economically irrelevant. It is not obvious to the citizen that the owner of a piece of property needed for community improvement is entitled to raise the price as high as possible. Nor can he readily sympathize with the management of a corporation that decides to lay off hundreds of workers and defends its action on economic grounds.

If sacrificing of noneconomic values to economic ones bothers the citizen, the notion that honesty doesn't pay; that a sense of duty is irrelevant to economic arguments; that to do more than obey the letter of the law is naive and foolish, is even more troublesome. And this uneasiness is not altogether a matter of moral sentiment. Virtue does have a money value, vice has a money price, and the prices are not insignificant. For example, it is estimated that $176 billions of taxable income is regularly unreported, and that although the efforts of the IRS are themselves costly, they do not effectively reduce illegal tax evasion. The figures for the costs of preventing and punishing arson, robbery, illegal traffic in drugs, and gambling, not to mention shoplifting, are also available. One must add their depredations to the costs of the goods and services the citizen consumes or tries to consume. All these costs are ultimately passed on to consumers. To make a business profitable they have to be.

Part of the cost, of course, could be obviated by decriminalizing crime. That would free the market from such noneconomic factors as law and morality; but without these restraints, there would be no market at all. We would have general reciprocal depredation—a state of nature that Hobbes postulated as the original condition of mankind. Suppose one were to ask what economic resources would be saved if individual citizens were morally upright and tried to act fairly and justly with each other and in accordance with the laws of the land. The question is complicated by the fact that even ill-gotten gains produce positive economic effects on the flow of goods and services. Bank robbers spend their loot in respectable stores, and the embezzler's investment is as effective as the honest investor's. Police and firefighters' jobs would be jeopardized if all human beings were law abiding. The question must therefore be expanded to ask whether the depredations of vice and crime reduce the total available pool of goods and services or merely redistribute them "unfairly."

Clearly some forms of immoral behavior produce more ill than good. Arson, the drug traffic, murder, and attacks that result in permanent bodily injury are ill winds that blow more harm than good. Furthermore, crime and other forms of antisocial behavior necessitate diversion of labor and skill from productive occupations to preventive or punitive ones (e.g, firefighting, police). The insurance business, for example, insofar as it covers loss of property and health through crime, uses large pools of manpower and capital that 'might be used elsewhere. All of which supports the common citizen's intuition that crime, or the absence of virtue, carries a large economic price tag. It is safe to conjecture that, despite the good that the ill wind of criminal activity inadvertently blows to the virtuous citizen, the economic costs of vice outweigh the incidental benefits it may bring about.

The cure, according to orthodox faith in the economic incentive, is to make crime economically unattractive. One might argue that if law is strictly and efficiently enforced, crime will not pay; but if strict enforcement becomes expensive, then the community "cannot afford it." If the police force makes the economic incentive primary (for its own operation)—and presumably they would be economic fools if they did not—the cost of law enforcement could conceivably become economically unsound.

Or it might be argued that even if crime does pay, it doesn't pay as well as honest work. Yet the citizen reads daily that gains through crime are swifter, larger, and often safer than in ordinary law-abiding activities. It is difficult to imagine a highly complex capitalist society in which the economic incentive to crime would not be high, especially if the risk of detection and punishment is reduced by fraud, bribery, and collusion with the authorities. Organized crime is already a feature of the modern free enterprise society and often is so intertwined with legitimate business as to render the moral question moot.

Our economic system creates a vested interest in crime, not only on the part of the wrongdoers but on the thousands whose livelihood depends on them. The construction industry can use building contracts for prisons, and lawyers need criminals—as do the police. Crime is a source of income for many people who may disapprove of crime and do their best to combat it, as well as to the lawbreaker who derives a direct benefit from it. Once crime is institutionalized by professional careers devoted to dealing with it, it also becomes part of the economic system. In a society committed to the dominance of economic incentives, it becomes difficult to distinguish crime for profit from production for profit; it is therefore not uncommon to find crime syndicate figures operating legitimate business and industrial enterprises in symbiosis with illegitimate ones.

The credibility of a social/economic theory that makes all activity depend on economic incentives is not high. Just as the enforcement of law depends on most people obeying the law voluntarily because it is the *right* thing to do, so does the economic life of a society, including a capitalistic, free market one, depend on the faith that most citizens are acting on more incentives that are not economic and that in critical instances moral incentives will override them. The economic costs of immorality imply economic benefits of virtue. The task of a good society is not to separate morality from the marketplace but rather to see to it that virtue is not only its own reward.

REFERENCES

1. Hilton Kramer, speculating on the effect of J. Paul Getty's fortune, which supports an art museum in Malibu Beach, California, notes that it could outbid every conceivable rival, not only for works of art, but for the services of scholars, curators, and conservators. *New York Times*, 10 August 1980.

2. *New York Times*, 10 May 1980.

3. Bertrand de Jouvenal, "Back to Basics," *Futurist* 14 (June 1980): 11.

4. An excellent illustration of this can be found in Robert L. Heilbronner's review of *A Guide to Post-Keynesian Economics*, ed. Alfred S. Eichner (White Plains, N.Y.: M.E. Sharpe, 1979). His attempt to explain the current debates in economic theory is clear enough to a reader already familiar with this sort of literature, and supports the charge that economics is not only dismal but hardly a science. In explicating the post-Keynesian theories, even Heilbronner's clarifying powers outrun the capacities of the well-intentioned layman. *New York Review of Books* 27 (21 February 1980): 19–22.

5. The year of the Jubilee when, according to the Old Testament, slaves were freed and all land was returned to its original tribal owners. Even then it was clear that the strong and shrewd would get control of the patrimony of the less competitive tribes.

6. Albert T. Sommers, quoted in *Wall Street Journal*, 9 October 1979, p. 24.

7. Paul Johnson, *Enemies of Society* (New York: Atheneum, 1977), p. 69. The moral aspect of Marxism goes beyond economic theory. It lies at the root of

the distinction between Marxism as a theory of revolution and a description of historical and economic determinism. For discussions bearing on the controversy, see Peter Singer's review of the following books in the *New York Review of Books* 27, no. 14 (25 September 1980): 62 ff: David McLellan, *Marxism After Marx* (New York: Harper & Row, 1980); Alvin W. Gouldner, *The Two Marxisms: Contradictions and Anomalies in the Development of Theory* (New York: Continuum Books/ Seabury Press, 1980); Stanley Moore, *Marx on the Choice Between Socialism and Communism* (Cambridge, Mass.: Harvard University Press, 1980); Paul Thomas, *Karl Marx and the Anarchists* (London: Routledge & Kegan Paul, 1980); and Robert L. Heilbronner, *Marxism: For and Against* (New York: W.W. Norton, 1980).

8. Shlomo Maital, "Inflation: It's Time for Controls," *New York Times*, 13 January 1980.

9. Courtney C. Brown, *Beyond the Bottom Line* (New York: Macmillan, 1979).

10. These sciences, including political science, jurisprudence, management, and administration, have been called "regulative sciences." *See* Joseph T. Tykociner, *Research as a Science—Zetetics*, (Urbana, Ill., 1959), pp. 31 ff.

11. *See* H.S. Broudy, "Criteria for a Humane Society," *Educational Studies* 8 (1977): 37–50.

12. "Two Pleas at Berkeley," *New York Review of Books* 27, no. 12 (17 July 1980): 25.

13. Royall Brandis, "Future Imperfect" *Quarterly Review of Economics and Business* 20, no. 2 (Summer 1980): 100. *See* also his *Economics: Principles and Policies* (Homewood, Ill.: R.D. Irwin, 1959).

14. I have tried to deal with this problem in "Criteria for a Humane Society." *See* also John Rawls, *A Theory of Justice* (Cambridge, Mass.: Belknap Press, 1971).

7

Other Strains on Credibility

In previous chapters a variety of threats to credibility was discussed. Academics and professionals have endangered credibility insofar as specialism has led them to attenuate the natural contexts of their problems.

Another, somewhat mixed, assortment of issues and attitudes also creates credibility gaps. One of these is a claim to moral superiority by virtue of loyalty to principle, a claim often supported by a brave and unpopular stand on a particular social issue. Because the erosion of credibility can be traced to a willingness to sacrifice principle for selfish interests, to lose credibility because of adherence to principle presents an interesting anomaly.

Typical is the following: Judge X, concurring with the arguments of the American Civil Liberties Union, finds for the defendant in an especially messy pornography case because the First Amendment guarantees freedom of speech. Better that a pornographer, whom the judge and the ACLU say they despise, go free and be allowed to corrupt the young—as the judge admits may happen—than to abridge freedom of expression. This is typical of situations in which officials or organizations defend procedurely what they substantively disapprove on grounds of principle. Similar stands have been taken to permit Nazi and Ku Klux Klan groups to hold public meetings.

The situation discomfits even the most sophisticated among us, for there should not be so sharp a discrepancy between our sentiments and our principles. Either the sense of outrage with the pornographer is misguided and ought to be suppressed or the construal of the principle is somehow faulty· and absolute loyalty to it unwarranted. There is something wrong in a culture that harbors such discrepancies.

The usual recourse in such a contretemps is to redefine terms. We ask anew, What does freedom of speech mean? The redefinitional ploy almost never succeeds; it removes one ambiguity by creating many more; it displaces one loophole with many. General principles like the Ten Commandments or the Bill of Rights are responses to what at the time of their being written into constitutions and on stone tablets were generally regarded as dangers to great goods, especially to the public good. The First Amendment on freedom of speech was a response to the danger that a despotic government would make criticism of it too dangerous to be undertaken. It was also regarded as essential for rational determination of the common good. The Ten Commandments were clearly exhortations in behalf of necessary virtues or prohibitions of generally recognized evils. Broad principles ignore a thousand particular variations of circumstances that characterize real life, and especially the strong probability that every such principle can and will be abused. Outrage or moral indignation results when they are abused with impunity. At such times we are more aware of the social harm and injustice caused by the abuse of the principle than the presumptive benefits that its proper use is intended to yield. To exchange actual harm for possible and abstract benefits goes against common sense and against the moral sense as well, for the doctrinaire adherence to an abstraction condones harm to actual innocent victims and creates an obligation to prevent it.

The strongest argument in favor of absolute loyalty to principle is that to limit it in unworthy cases would invite limiting it in worthy ones as well. Thus, punishing the pornographer may deprive society of a great poet or a reformer. Genius has a way of bursting out of even the strongest chains, but it seems reasonable to believe that, on the whole, freedom is in the best interests of mankind, despite the dangers, while to inhibit and to chill genius is not. This is so because the genius is often out of tune with the times and not recognized as being ahead of them. We have to gamble that some doctrines offensive to currently accepted sentiments will in the future become congruent with sentiment; history seems to have vindicated the gamble.

Some of the anomalies resulting from absolute loyalty to or disregard of principle can be mitigated by raising the credibility question, namely, by asking whether the proponents of the principle are willing to bear the costs of its abuse. Would the defenders of *Miranda*, (the legal ruling that defines the rights of a person when placed under arrest) no matter what, be willing to reimburse out of their own purse the victims of criminals who invoke *Miranda* successfully to escape punishment? Would the

National Rifle Association, which in the name of the (misinterpreted) right of the citizen to bear arms fights every effort to control the sale of handguns, be willing to pay damages to the victims of handgun murders and their survivors?

To be sure, the credibility test does not determine the validity of the principles involved. So long as the principle remains in the realm of abstract argument, no test of credibility is needed, for one can entertain many principles without risk or cost. But when commitment to the principle impinges on existential territory and creates existential innocent victims, then the credibility test measures the sincerity of the parties at issue and comes closer to satisfying the demands of justice and equity. Adherence to principle at any cost—to others—is not a mark of moral heroism.

Another example of the need for the credibility test in commitment to principle is the application of the civil and human rights legislation of the 1960s. Especially vulnerable is the interpretation of the legislation that liberates individuals from constraints on private conduct. Victimless "crimes," for example, such as the taking of drugs, sexual activity (between consenting adults), and unconventional sexual preferences were not to be forbidden and overt marks of disapproval of such conduct were proscribed—in some cases by law.

THE PRICE OF LIBERATION

The heady feeling of liberation often obscures some of its consequences and not to take account of them impairs the credibility of militant liberationists. For examples, rarely does doing one's thing take full account of consequences to others, albeit in principle, exercising freedom entails the responsibility not to infringe on the freedom of others. Are there, for example, really victimless crimes, which on that account ought not to be called crimes and therefore be permitted? The taking of harmful drugs, prostitution, sexual "perversions," and flaky behavior in general, it is sometimes argued, hurt nobody but their practitioner—if they hurt at all—and ought not to be proscribed by any law. But can any of us cut our connections with members of our family, our friends, the people who depend on us, so clearly and completely that what we do does not have consequences for them? The right to privacy is limited by the possibility of privacy.

Furthermore, there is much in the liberationist movements, individual or collective, that operates on the assumption that not only should one be free to do one's thing but that it shall be done with impunity so far as the disapproval of others is concerned. By some strange alchemy, the expression of disapproval, even when not physical, is taken by the exerciser of freedom as an offense against freedom. By what principle is the right to be offended by the distasteful action of others and to dislike them abridged? True, the law forbids certain expressions of that disapproval and dislike, but many forms of legal and covert reprisal can be as damaging as the more overt kind. Social ostracism is one example; it can be a bitter reprisal indeed. The principles of individual freedom protect adherence to the mores of the group as well as revolt against them.

The right to free speech, assembly, petition, and so forth does not entail the duty to exercise these rights. The right to marches and demonstrations does not command anyone to exercise that right, and there may be circumstances when to exercise it would entrain consequences (e.g., extensive bloodshed) that far outweigh the benefits. Under such circumstances, it would be right to refrain from demonstrating and wrong not to do so. The moral quality of an action is not established only by a formal right to perform it. The right to say what one thinks need not be exercised at a friendly dinner party, and neighborliness often excludes behavior that we have a right to perform. Seemliness (civility) is hard to define, but actions that are unseemly *prima facie* need to make a case for their performance that overrides the unseemliness.

Liberationists who are sincere in their loyalty to the principle at all costs can demonstrate that sincerity by accepting without complaint the consequences of exercising their freedom. The credibility of reformers, protestors, and militant advocates of good causes is seriously compromised when they insist not only on the right to attack this or that establishment but to escape retaliation from those whom they provoke. Legally they may be in the right, and oblige police to protect them, but only from physical interference within well-defined limits. Their good sense and sincerity become suspect if they expect or demand that those whom they attack will refrain from retaliation.

In the 1979–80 troubles with Iran over the hostages, the rights of the Iranian students in this country to demonstrate against the United States and not to be deported were protected by the courts. But the Iranian students, not yet citizens, violated civility when they failed to behave as guests should, and this understandably provoked hostility. Not to resent the rudeness of uninvited guests is neither reasonable nor credible. People who "rise above" such impulses are likely to lose their credibility; if they are sincere, then they are apparently incapable of appropriate feelings; and if they are not sincere, they are hypocrites. And their credibility is further impaired if what the Iranian protestors or unhappy refugees do to disturb the peace injures others, not the defenders of principle.

The only unqualified good, Immanuel Kant said, is a good will, that is a will determined solely by the sense of duty, of right and wrong. This is formal rightness, which is judged by the intention of the agent. An action can have good or evil consequences, however, and these determine its material rightness, or lack of it. To be completely moral, an act has to be right both formally and materially. I may give a dollar to a beggar with the best and purest of intentions, to relieve him of suffering, and I may do so not merely because I sympathize with suffering, but because it is a duty to relieve suffering whenever possible. Yet if that dollar is spent in such a way as to harm the beggar, my action may be materially wrong.

The use of freedom is no exception. All morality hinges on the possibility of freedom to choose. In that sense and as subjective satisfaction, freedom is an unqualified good. Nevertheless, the use of freedom is an act judged by the intention of the agent and its consequences for everyone concerned. These are platitudes, to be sure, but attention to some consequences of freedom needs to be drawn at a time when doing as one pleases is regarded by so many as an unqualified good. Of these, perhaps the most overlooked and serious is the potential isolation of the individual who asserts or claims it. If A declares freedom from B, B may also choose to become free from A. Thus if A is being attacked by hoodlums, B's intervention is hard for A to demand. At that moment, B helps A, not because he owes it to A, but because he respects the personhood and humanity of A. The principle that one has a right to do what one pleases provided it does not injure another is insufficient to command the aid of another. The consequences of social independence are momentous. The network of family, neighborhood, and community loyalties is the binding medium of mutual aid, not the abstract principles used to explicate and rationalize it. Not a little of the apparent indifference to victims of violence by those who witness it may be the result of taking the injunction to mind their own business literally. When this cocoon syndrome becomes endemic, the social network of mutual aid is destroyed. Only a higher principle of moral obligation sustains it.

ADVOCACY AND CREDIBILITY

Much of the social and intellectual ferment of the last decade resulted in an intoxication with freedoms and rights. Various groups battled for equality of legal and psychological rights for women, children, homosexuals, minorities, and political dissidents here and abroad. The citizen is asked formally or informally to decide politically as well as morally whether or not to grant these claims. On what grounds can the citizen make a rational decision?

Such controversies have something odd about them. For on the face of it, why should rights not be distributed equally to all members of the body politic? Why should they be denied and why should it be necessary to legislate such equality? The answers vary, of course. Blacks and Indians have to fight for rights that had been historically denied them. Some minorities may have been denied certain rights because they had not entered the country legally. Certain rights of women and children have traditionally been limited by codes governing marriage and inheritance. Some rights, however, have been denied by custom and customary belief as to what has been decreed by nature or Supernature. The rights of women to participate in men's sports and the rights of homosexuals are familiar examples of the latter type of denial.

On abstract grounds of rational principle it is difficult to justify opposition to equal rights. The persistent opposition in certain quarters as well as the insistent demands for them in other quarters raise questions of credibility. Is the opposition the result of fear of competition or of losing privileges and advantages? Where self-esteem depends on presumptive superiority over some class of persons, the prospect of losing that superiority is threatening. For example, men who rely on superiority of physical strength for security and self-esteem are bothered by the prospect of women becoming athletic or able to tackle jobs requiring physical strength and agility. Many concrete conditions foster opposition to granting rights to a group heretofore without them, but these "causes" are likely to be suppressed in debate in favor of "good" reasons.

A more sincere opposition to equalizing rights is grounded in an implicit reluctance to disturb customary roles and functions in the social order. At any given time the division of labor and status is taken for granted by all concerned, and this makes life predictable. To change the distribution of privileges, status, and roles disrupts stability, and this may be feared even by those who do not stand to lose personally by the change. And whatever the proposed or imposed changes, even some of the putative beneficiaries may prefer to forego them. Much of the opposition to certain legislation for women's rights comes from women.

The supervening principle in the quarrels is the right of choice. It is left to the woman, for example, to take advantage of new freedoms or to pass them by. While eminently rational and sensible on abstract grounds, this principle overlooks the difficulty of implementing the right of choice. For choices have social consequences and women who have felt quite comfortable in traditional sexual roles are not grateful for being turned into revolutionaries to preserve or destroy the old order.

Advocacy of rights on principle is more credible when no personal advantage is gained thereby and when the advocate is willing to bear the consequences of the advocacy. Thus to champion rights for certain groups who will endanger the jobs of some people but not of the advocate impugns the purity of the advocacy, however rational and right the principle.

Credibility is also threatened when the advocate's behavior seems incompatible with the claim to certain rights. For example, when female employees campaign and sue for the right to be free from sexual harassment on the job and from reprisals from superiors when sexual advances are rejected, it is hard to find any reasonable argument against it. On all grounds of decency and morality, the case seems to be clear-cut. Why, then, do some citizens, both male and female, harbor reservations about laws and penalties to prevent it? It cannot be because they believe the female employee's sexual charms incite helpless male employees to make sexual advances, for this is no more justified than to blame a jewel's brilliance for its being stolen.

The reservations that otherwise logical and right-minded people harbor are not grounded in law or logic as much as in credibility. Instances are cited of females who dress and comport themselves so that they seem to be inviting advances. The inference is drawn that such females are never "harassed" by sexual advances, but rather welcome them. These instances are taken as justification for a general skepticism about the sincerity of those who campaign against harassment. What would convince them to believe otherwise? Would dressing in chadors be acceptable evidence of sincerity? In China, we are told, working clothes do not accentuate sexual allure. Would the foes of harassment also advocate such desexualizing uniforms?

The situation is complicated by the fact that in their zeal for equality and liberation from being regarded as sex objects, women forget that they *are* sex objects, just as males *are*. Anatomically, cosmetically, and sartorially, the sex characteristics are marked and often emphasized. Yet persons are supposed not to react to these sexual characteristics in the workplaces. Forbidding overt reactions does not abolish the covert ones, nor does the fact that most people do not overtly react to sexual objects sexually change the sex object into a nonsexual one.

Should the citizen take credibility into account? Yes, if the measure being advocated involves consequences and costs that have to be borne by the body politic or by innocent parties. It touches on issues of practical and substantive justice; on the delicate balance between abstract justice and concrete injustice, so that in actual controversies over legislation the question of fairness becomes relevant.

The willingness or unwillingness of the claimant of a right to sacrifice something for it is a mark of credibility. Or, to put it another way, advocacy of a policy on the grounds of principle is judged not only on the rightness of the principle or on the logic of its claims but also on whether the cost of granting the claim will be borne by the advocates as well as by others, that is, fairly distributed.

The notion of fairness also entails that the person asked to make the sacrifice have an adequate opportunity to acquiesce in it, that it be not arbitrarily imposed by the will of others—even by the will of constituted authorities. This right entrains the right to inquire whether the sacrifice is necessary and whether it is fairly distributed.

Whether or not the sacrifice is fair in these senses is a matter of truth about circumstances that in principle, at least, can be ascertained in some verifiable fashion. Legislative hearings on taxation might serve as examples of truth-seeking inquiries of this kind. But in these situations it is also pertinent and proper to ask: How do the proponents of this measure, urged in behalf of the public good, stand to benefit from its passage? How much of the cost are they *as individuals* ready to assume?

In recent years many of the affirmative action proposals have been most vigorously urged by persons who will not bear their cost, but on the contrary may very well reap professional and political benefits from them, albeit the measure is for the benefit of others (e.g., minorities, women). It has been remarked cynically that if the politicians had to be on the firing lines, there would be few wars. Similarly, if proponents of social reform of the Left or the Right were forbidden to profit personally from the measures, or charged with their costs, there would be a drastic reduction in the lobbying industry.

These are issues of credibility, not of truth, for it is quite possible that the merits of a proposal are just as their advocates state, whether or not they themselves stand to profit from them. That as ordinary citizens, and not as logicians, we mix the truth and credibility issues is owing to the adhesive and cohesive nature of social phenomena. And because history argues against the credibility of interested parties when they purport to argue solely from the merits of political issues, it behooves the ordinary citizen to be wary of such arguments.

Whose ox is being gored, whose ax is being ground, who will bear the costs and who will reap the benefits are all relevant questions that in part can be answered by the truth, but more often in our times must be judged on their credibility.

RELATIVISM AND CREDIBILITY

Many of the most strident advocates of liberation ground their protest against the established order on the principle of relativism. The doctrine that all values and norms are relative to the culture or the group or the individual was enunciated long ago by Protagoras, who proclaimed that man is the measure of all things. This denied Divine origin to norms. However, he pointed out that not every individual man is the measure; that only the wise man is. Cultural relativism taken literally argues that there is no set of values that all individuals are constrained by nature or logic to accept. The principle has been expanded to allow the individual to make his own codes of value and to change them whenever impelled to do so. The principle is intended to emancipate us from the oppression of social constraints imposed in the name of universal laws. Nevertheless, that an accepted code of conduct is not sanctioned by natural or supernatural law does not free the individual from the consequences of rejecting it. Relativism is no panacea for the constraints of social life.

As a general principle, relativism is self-defeating, both logically and strategically. Logically, it is self-contradictory, for if nothing is absolutely true, then this principle is no exception. Strategically, the force of the principle is to free action from the constrictions of absolutes. However, relativizing all claims to truth frees all claims from criticism or question; that is, it absolutizes them. The price of relativism is the multiplication of absolutes.

Thoroughgoing relativism probably is rarely taken seriously as a working principle, but the press for liberation of recent times seems to have elevated it to that status. The cult of narcissism, freedom in sexual preferences, the relativizing of sex differences in all aspects of life, and a half hundred other revolts against authority in the name of individual or human rights are all held to be justified by the denial of any absolute truth or principle to the contrary. Situational ethics puts ethics at the mercy of situational interpretation, and is binding on no one.

A sensible relativism does not deny constants. It uses them only to limit questioning to certain contexts. When playing chess, the rules are not to be questioned; within a theological system, some tenets are not put into question. Such limitations of context make rational debate possible and permit rational decisions within each context. But it often does preclude a confrontation of two or more contexts on a theoretical plane. The rules of chess tell us nothing about the rules of law or theology or marital fidelity. Yet it is precisely when two systems or contexts collide that the most serious problems of rational action arise.

Procedural relativisim cuts up the seamless web of existential relevance into domains that are held to be independent of each other. For example, in the recent flouting of American supremacy by small and relatively underdeveloped nations long-range consideration of economic and political advantage was severed from the emotional commitment of the citizenry to national honor. The debate over foreign policy in Iran, the Middle East, and Afghanistan was between two kinds of context commitment. Shrewd pragmatists who had the advantage of this country at heart wanted to exclude moral considerations as irrelevant. The "gut" people were willing to risk advantage for the moral and psychological satisfaction of revenge and retaliation.

Procedural relativism, therefore, is a useful working principle for rational action so long as the several contexts can be kept apart. Unfortunately, in matters of social import, separation of contexts often results in their confrontation. The pragmatists and the moralists in national policy sooner or later come into conflict on military expenditures, embargos, treaties, and the like. It is not always possible for diverse contexts to live and let live behind high fences. Matters of great social import are rarely amenable to the logical scalpel, as has been pointed out many times in this book. That a tax policy will reinvigorate savings and investment at the expense of social services does not lend itself to a neat dissection of relevance into economic growth on one side and social justice on the other. Single-issue politics fragment the relevance fabric to the point where they lose their own relevance and become petty.

MEDIA AND CREDIBILITY

The extraordinary revolution in communication effected by electronic technology is supposed to be a boon to rational action. For one thing, it makes more information available to more people; for another, it makes it available almost instantaneously. Has action, individual or civic, become more rational? Has almost continuous polling on virtually all issues increased the rationality of our decisions?

If one points to the continued controversy over issues as negative evidence, then it is retorted that these are issues over which reasonable persons can differ. But what causes the difference? Some of the answers have already been suggested, namely, that the alleged knowledge or facts or truths do not coincide, and what is more often the case, the truth serves diverse interests differently.

The electronic media development adds further complications to the well-intentioned citizen's efforts to act on the basis of the best available knowledge. The speed factor in mass news reporting necessitates selection from the "facts," and that selection is not guided by the need for completeness, fairness, or subtlety. It is guided by the newsworthiness (general interest) of an event and the form of its presentation. In addition, the media package a mixture of opinion and news. The consumer knows no more about the ingredients than he does about the constituents of packaged foods.

As one example of the self-defeating results of the electronic technology, consider the so-called panel interview in which newspersons "grill" a notable for half an hour or so, interspersed by high-minded commercials. These shows, and they are shows, are widely heralded as an aid to bringing, if not truth, then at least clarification on major issues to a public thirsting for enlightenment.

A typical format brings a high government official before the panel of questioners. The show proceeds somewhat as follows:

Interviewer: Is it true that we are in a recession, Mr. Secretary?

Mr. Secretary: That depends on what you mean by a recession, does it not?

Interviewer: Well, is the unemployment going to exceed nine percent by January 1?

Mr. Secretary: We hope not.

Interviewer: Then you are afraid it might?

Mr. Secretary: I didn't say that.

Interviewer: But if you're not afraid, why do you rely on hope?

Mr. Secretary: This is a great country; we are a hopeful people.

Interviewer: Will the President introduce a tax cutting bill if unemployment persists at the nine percent level?

Mr. Secretary: We shall follow our policy of watching developments carefully and taking appropriate action at the appropriate time.

Interviewer: Thank you, Mr. Secretary.

Interviews of this kind resemble the adversarial maneuvers of the courtroom. Reporters try to make somebody say something significant —preferably scandalous—that the interviewee does not want to reveal; otherwise there would be little point to the interview in the first place. If the interviewee wanted to reveal something, it could be done better by a news release or official announcement; what is known in the trade as a "handout." When the interviewee is a government or high corporate official, the outcome is predictable. Unless drunk, hypnotized, or in the grip of overpowering resentment against superiors, he or she will tell anything but the whole truth, albeit nothing said will be false. No amount of badgering, needling, and cleverness will drive the interviewee from the protection of ambiguity, hair splitting, and equivocation. Why, then, does the official consent to be interviewed? The answer lies in the need for the agency to maintain visibility with the public and good public relations with the media.

This kind of interviewing, undertaken to inform the public on important issues, is futile for at least two reasons. One is that the rules of the game demand a hide-and-seek format, to give it some of the excitement of a contest or conflict. The interviewee is committed to frustrating the interviewer, and therewith the viewer as well. The other is that as long as the questions are about matters of policy and future actions, no important agency can afford to be explicit and candid. There are too many contingencies, too many interests waiting to take advantage of advance information, and too many dangers of creating opposition prematurely. Diplomacy, sometimes characterized as the art of lying for one's country (or firm), may be necessary, but is it necessary to carry it on in interview programs?

Inasmuch as the radio-television channels are "leased" by the people to the media, programs such as "Meet the Press," "Face the Nation," and "Issues and Answers" are a scandalous waste of communication resources. Documentaries tend to be dull, but they do give information and expert opinion; interviews create neither good drama nor information. Although these "shows" are scheduled so as not to interfere with the viewer's preoccupation with sex, violence, and football games, they let the dutiful citizen hoping for enlightenment down. The effect on the general credibility of the mass media is deplorable.

CHECKING CREDIBILITY AND TRUTH

When credibility is in doubt, the effort to get at the truth is formalized. In gang culture, the procedure is torture, or the threat of torture. The usual method in other establishments is to check the statements of those whose credibility is in question. Sometimes this takes the form of examining appropriate documents, as when there is suspicion of financial shenanigans. Or one set of official reports may be used to check on other official reports. Investigating committees employ devices of this kind as well as cross-examination of witnesses. The number of such investigations, judging by the number publicized, must be substantial. As might be expected, checking, investigating, and evading the investigators has become professionalized with credibility problems of their own.

One elaborate form of checking is called evaluation or accountability. Here the goal is not to unmask liars and cheaters, but to arrive at estimates of an enterprise's success in fulfilling its promises or goals. Legislative and educational programs are frequently the subject of evaluations by experts of one kind or another, because they suffer from an almost *a priori* lack of credibility with respect to efficiency. The controversial nature of government social service programs makes them favorite targets for evaluation. The opponents of all such programs would have the public believe that they are no more than "boondoggles" designed to rob the rich in order to "pamper" the improvident poor, and to provide jobs for bureaucrats. Many programs designed to implement the civil rights legislation of the 1960s on equality of educational and economic opportunities for minorities have been evaluated as "making no appreciable difference." Some have been upgraded by subsequent evaluations.

Evaluation procedures when applied internally by the participants themselves are supposed to improve the understanding of the project and help locate strong and weak points. Benign, nonthreatening evaluation is supposed to serve as an instrument of self-education and self-reform. When applied by outsiders, it becomes a species of accounting to promote accountability, diagnosis of defects, and a search for remedies. Evaluation by an external team removes, or is supposed to allay, suspicion of self-serving judgments and to enhance credibility.

The flaw in this ointment—and the evaluative jargon as it is professionalized can become oleaginous indeed—is that the evaluation enterprise in general is itself open to questions of credibility both as to procedural competence and purity of motive. As to competence, reliability of judgment varies from very high, when the criteria are highly objective, easily identified, observed and measured, to very low, when the phenomena being judged are ill defined, imbedded in dense contexts, and loaded with intangibles. Social and educational enterprises tend to cluster in the latter reaches of the spectrum of reliability, validity, and credibility. One hazard is that "social inquiry is being steered, increasingly, by the methodological tools available, not by the fundamental questions being asked . . . methodologies are focussing more and more on the fragments that yield to quantitative measures and analyses, inducing policy makers to focus attention on the trees, and lose sight of the forest."[1]

Accordingly, in educational evaluation, styles of data gathering and processing become standardized as the evaluation industry expands into large-scale production. School testing for evaluation and accountability is now big business.

There is also the credibility of the evaluators themselves. It was inevitable when evaluation became part of virtually every research and development grant that a professional class of evaluation specialists would emerge. And, as with other specializations, this one would also formalize its procedures, invent a technical terminology, and substitute procedural purity for substantive issues. As a result, much of the energy and funds allotted for evaluation goes into procedures and the invention of devices to monitor the monitors of the monitors. The current controversies over school testing are familiar examples. "Evaluators are no more prone to bite the hand that feeds them than any other group of persons concerned about their own well being. Since governmental agencies account for most of the support for evaluation, there is no pecuniary return for doing critical evaluation of their own supporters."[2]

The futile efforts to detect and prevent waste and corruption in government are altogether too familiar. Less familiar, and one might hope less futile, are analogous procedures to ensure that research and educational projects are funded impartially according to merit and carried out as promised. This has eventuated in a new occupation, proposal writing, an important component of the grantsmanship industry. The money and time spent on this activity is worth careful scrutiny; especially when so much of it is invested on the supposition that panels of experts will award grants and projects solely on the merits of the evidence submitted by the proposal writers. The relation between success in being funded and merit has become so attenuated that failure is no longer taken as a sign of professional inadequacy; one merely writes more proposals and hopes for better luck next time.

A colleague of mine, an economist by trade, has estimated that a good deal more of the money earmarked for research by the granting agencies would be spent on research if the awards were made by a lottery than by the existing evaluation procedures. For one thing, these procedures soak up a lot of the funds that might go into research activity; for another, he doubts—although it is heresy to say so—that there is a high degree of correlation between evaluation procedures and the quality of projects funded.

Despite the difficulties, any set of ratings of schools, colleges, departments, and social agencies is greeted warmly by the public and respected by the trade. Numbers, ordinal or cardinal, have an invincible innocence that makes it difficult to believe that they could be lying; they have high credibility. Reading scores, when reported on a municipal or state basis, have more effect on educational policy and expenditures than a dozen think tanks devoted to study these matters.

Universities are rated by various organizations for research excellence, general excellence, academic excellence, student excellence, financial excellence, and every other index of merit that some rating group can think up. These ratings are eagerly noted. The winners preen themselves, and the losers use their low ratings to get more funds to improve them. Numbers not only have high credibility but spare administrators the need for a more substantive understanding of an educational institution and its quality. The private reservations that educators and politicians may have about ratings give way to their usefulness in public relations.

There is nothing fundamentally wrong with formal evaluation, and probably any systematic attempt to evaluate a product or a process is better than none. Nor does it pay to destroy confidence in evaluation. It only encourages the incompetent to become more so. But there is an unseemly naiveté about the attempt to convert the subjective into the objective by incantation of numbers. And there is the danger of destroying the phenomena in the conversion.

Human good is as variable as the domains of human value, which in their entanglement encompass the human condition. Much of that condition, perhaps most of it, is the product of imagination, thought, and language. Some of these products have achieved a high degree of order (e.g., the sciences and the diverse intellectual disciplines). In these orderly fields, evaluation can also be highly ordered. Other "products," such as aspirations, dreams, satisfactions and frustrations, unities and disunities of self, are not highly ordered and cannot be evaluated as if they were. In between there are other grades and kinds of order. Art, for example, is an ordering as well as a creative principle.

To evaluate the human realities requires not only being one but also a peculiarly human insight into them. Scholars within an intellectual discipline, for example, develop an intuitive connoisseurship for judging quality within that discipline. The intuitive resources have been built up and sorted out by long years of fine discrimination of a rich store of particulars. The input, so to speak, ferments, and the distillate is literally an extract, a flavoring that is clearly discerniable to the expert, but only vaguely, if at all, to the uninitiated. The scholarly guilds by their rules of entry build these criteria into their certified members so that they can judge a program, a publication, a department with a high degree of reliability—as long as a standard sample of the discipline is the target of judgment.

Out of these disciplinary, intuitive criteria emerge reputational norms, so that "everybody knows" that institution A is "distinguished" in this discipline and that institution B would like to be but can't quite make it yet. If asked to break down these reputational judgments into measures of faculty, students, library, and publications, they can do so. A visiting team invited to evaluate a department will spend several days perusing faculty *vitae*, entrance requirements, library facilities, faculty publications, and other data put together in huge volumes of "self-study" materials. The criteria for a "good" faculty member, or a "good" publication, or a "good" library are themselves reputational, however. They are what highly reputed members of a discipline say is "good." If guildspeople, who are by definition "distinguished," are asked to evaluate an institution, the resultant ratings reflect their general and largely intuitive judgment rather than the procedures concocted to provide "objective" measures of quality. If the latter were to give a "distinguished" institution a low rating, the criteria, not the institution, would be discredited.

Evaluation on reputational criteria by people of reputation enjoys high credibility. Whether the more mechanized procedures do is less certain. The latter tend to encounter credibility problems themselves, because the adequacy of the procedures can be questioned. If experts of high repute are not used to evaluate the phenomena, then the procedures have to be so detailed that a layperson can use them. Expert winetasters and critics, for example, have made lists of qualities they consider criterial for quality in various types of wine. They have verbalized their own intuitive (reputational) criteria so that a nonexpert might make expert judgments. Any layperson who has tried to use these lists can testify that lists do not an expert make; a quality such as "fruitiness" is difficult for the layperson to identify. Is fruitiness "peachy," "plummy," or just "grapey?" Explicit product or process analyses do not improve the credibility of this kind of evaluation as much as one might expect.

No doubt the reader can think of other strains on credibility. Although they are caused by a variety of factors, two sets of circumstances give rise to most of them. One, of course, is the real or apparent incompatibility between diverse truth claims. This in itself troubles the citizenry precisely because it has great faith in experts. Disagreement among experts not only engenders doubts about their credibility but about the knowledge on which their expertise is built. The other circumstance, to be discussed in the next chapter, is the prevading de-valuation and de-moralization that accompanies specialization in the academic disciplines and the professions.

REFERENCES

1. Sar A. Levitan and Gregory Wurzburg, *Evaluating Federal Social Programs: An Uncertain Art* (Kalamazoo, Mich.: W.E. Upjohn Institute, 1979), p. 6

2. Ibid., p. 40.

8

Credibility and
De-Moralization

The previous chapters have been devoted largely to examples of the difficulties intelligent citizens encounter as they try to act rationally on matters of the public good. The case to be made was that warranted assertions on scientific or strictly intellectual grounds could not be relied upon to warrant belief and commitment.

These difficulties fall into two major categories. The more familiar one is that in a complex, interdependent, technologically dominated culture, the nonspecialist cannot assess rival and often incompatible truth claims made by experts. The second might be called de-valuation in its general form with de-moralization as a subspecies. De-valuation refers to diminishing or denying the relevance of all but one type of value to an issue; de-moralization denies the relevance of moral questions. The reduction of all values—intellectual, civic, health, among others—to a money value would be an example of de-valuation; the slogan "business is business" is an example of de-moralization.

Moral values are also regarded as supervalues used to adjudicate conflicting claims in other value areas. What and how we choose should conform to principles of formal and material rightness, and these are moral categories. We ought to choose in every conflict of value so as to maximize the good, however good is defined. To choose between giving a donation to a worthy charity and buying a fine painting, in this sense, is a moral choice. De-moralization, therefore, can refer to a general constriction of value contexts or to the neglect of the moral dimension in action

—a bothersome ambiguity. The use of the hyphen signifies the narrower use of the term.

DE-VALUATION

Logically, whether two statements are independent depends on whether the meaning of one entails the meaning of the other. For example, the concept of a body implies the concept of weight, and the concept of an angle implies the intersection of two lines. If this logical relation does not obtain between two concepts or ideas, then one concept can be entertained and uttered without necessarily uttering or entertaining the other. Thus David Hume argued that the concept of a cause does not imply a *necessary* connection between cause and effect, because he could think of one without thinking of the other, and he had no sense impression of any necessary connecting link between the two. The attempt to refute Hume furnished steady employment for subsequent philosophers. Based on this logical independence, or the claim to such independence, one can also argue for linguistic and psychological independence. A lawyer might insist that because one can talk about legal rules without mentioning justice or deny that *caveat emptor* has to include the mention of fairness, one can resist their intrusion into legal discussion. Specialists may claim that if they can study their own domain without mentioning other domains, they are excused from responsibility for those other domains.

Causal connections should not be confused with logical connections: "physically causative" with "logically entailed." Nor should lack of logical entailment be confused with causal independence. When a legalist insists that the rules of law do not entail the rules of justice and therefore justice issues need not be invoked, it may be replied that the ability to think of one without inference to the other does not mean that there is no causal relation between them. A sense of injustice can arouse (cause) indignant behavior, and the assertion that the judge's decision was legally correct, albeit unjust, may very well arouse even more palpable consequences. Psychological connections resist the logical knife.

The nonspecialist—outside of his specialty—does not engage in such acute analysis. Values are not compartmentalized. He does not think of business without thinking that one way of doing business is more fair to the customer than another. He cannot contemplate a criminal who has confessed to a brutal murder being let off because the confession was obtained under legally improper circumstances, without all sorts of emotions welling up and spilling over into his judgments. Accordingly, when law, business, medicine, or any other profession insists that it is free to ignore these existential value interpenetrations, it loses credibility on suspicion that logical tricks are being used to evade responsibility.

The fragmentation of the existential context of thought and action by the specialists forces the citizen to seek reintegrating strategies for himself. To counter de-valuation requires the restoration of the connections among the various value domains. This can be done on an educated or an uneducated basis. The conceptual-imagic flow with which we think and feel from moment to moment is itself an integrative mechanism. Some of it is free association, the laws of which remain a mystery, despite efforts to demystify it. Some of the integration is supplied by the norms of our reference group, or of the popular culture as dispensed by the mass media. "Everybody knows that welfare recipients don't want to work," for example, is a widely shared stereotype, but so is the judgment that "everybody knows that a degree from Harvard is better than one from the State University." That a judgment is the result of an unexamined community consensus does not mean that it is false or that it will turn out to be so upon rational inquiry. All it means is that at the moment it is not warranted by such inquiry.

The educated reintegration of values requires a knowledge of the several value domains, the conditions of their attainment, their relationships, their intrinsic and extrinsic properties. Presumably such knowledge and understanding is the province and promise of general or liberal education. This is the subject matter of the humanities and the sciences *when considered from the point of view of individual human life, not from the departmental perspectives in the university.* It is not surprising that as specialization in academia increased, that is, as disciplines in both the sciences and the humanities became more like professions (the profession of scholarship), the fortunes of liberal education declined among both professors and students. We shall return to this topic in chapters 10 and 11.

CONTENT AND IMPORT

Reintegrating fragmented value domains requires that the citizen extract import from content. Ideally, a phenomenon or a problem is adequately explained by a correct analysis of its necessary and sufficient conditions. Typically, when the citizenry face a social problem that is national in scope, there is an impulse to collect the relevant information and expert opinion. Articles are written, experts interviewed, hearings held, letters written to the editor. This is the democratic process in its enlightened form.

However, the "input," as the discussion is called, comes from many sources. As a fairly typical example of such a problem and the debating process, consider the question of whether we should increase or halt industrial growth in this country and perhaps on the planet as well. At an International Symposium on Science, Technology, and the Human Prospect, San Francisco, April 1979, Chauncey Starr challenged the factual validity of the assumption that resources are limited:

Technology provides increased efficiency in the conversion of resources to human uses. . . . So far, we have extracted only a small fraction of the store in the earth's crust. History also tells us that the apparently limited resources available to mankind in any one period of time become just a small fraction of the resources ultimately available to later generations because of the intervening contribution of science and technology . . .

and he cites availability of oil as an example.[1]

Moreover, the experts cannot agree as to whether the civilization-energy equation is valid. George Basalla argues that "the vast increases in energy consumption over the past few decades have not necessarily enhanced our chances of reaching a new stage of civilization. . . . The Elizabethans managed quite well without the steam engine to produce a culture that is admired throughout the world."[2]

We are caught in a tragic ambivalence toward science and technology. On the one hand, they are the triumph of our century; on the other, they threaten the very civilization they made possible. We have neither the knowledge nor power to manage it for continued growth and prosperity, nor the virtues to control its inequities and dangers. Eric Hoffer, the self-educated philosopher, blames the intellectuals: "No one had an inkling that anarchy, when it came, would originate not in the masses, but in violent minorities, including the minority of the educated. Everything that was said about the anarchic propensities of the masses fits perfectly with the behavior of students, professors, writers, artists and the hangers-on during the righteous 60s."[3]

The term "human prospect" in the title of the symposium is the central concern of the citizenry, and we find Alasdair MacIntyre noting that "the energy crisis is a crisis about our whole way of life and not just about energy,"[4] and that the "environmentalists in the present have sometimes been as untrammeled in endangering other people's jobs as industrialists in the past were in endangering other people's investments."[5]

It is doubtful, however, that the citizen reading these authoritative accounts of the problem of energy and growth will or can make a decision on the quality of the information furnished by the discussants. For the issue is what makes life good, worthy of our striving and sacrifice. This is a philosophical, ethical, metaphysical issue, not merely a scientific one. As the citizen reads the analyses of the experts, his mind and intellect weigh the arguments, but tacitly he is matching what he reads with an image or a concept of what is good and right, just and humane. The writer who shares this perspective is more credible than one who does not, even though the respective analyses may be equally valid.

If the citizen is not in the mood to act in accordance with the public good, then the information given by the "input" is sifted and evaluated by more or less enlightened self-interest, although such a ploy can also present ambiguities and perplexities. For example, how is a worker employed by an electric utility company living near its nuclear reactor to decide what is in his best interest?

Even questions of self-interest have to be decided on the credibility of those who promise to provide for such self-interest. The prosperous citizen may vote for the Republican party because he believes it is more interested in prosperous citizens than is the Democratic party. Or the laboring man may vote for Democrats in the belief, not the knowledge, that it is sympathetic to the cause of labor. There is no need to repeat the examples cited in the chapter dealing with the obstacles to rational action. As life situations become more complex, the information relevant to it becomes more specialized, more technical, more esoteric, and less useful as a guide to action.

Confusing as the calculation of the effects of an action or a policy might be on various interests and interest groups, the balancing of the effects of changes in one value domain on another is no less so. For example, aesthetic values as realized in works of fine art (however "fine" is to be defined) are generally regarded as desirable and precious, but relatively low in the order of necessities. How much of its resources should a community devote to the aesthetic values? Does it make sense for householders to spend time and money growing lawns that they mow down each week? A manicured lawn is the householder's contribution to the aesthetic quality of the environment; it contributes to a pleasant prospect for neighbors and passersby. Are such rituals economically defensible? Real estate appraisers seem to think so.

An enterprising sales executive can rise more rapidly in his field if he is willing to move frequently from one region to another. His family is upset by the moves, and tensions within the family rise. Which value is the more important? Will not the increased salary furnish the family with more value potential in other domains: in health, recreation, travel, education?

Art museums, theaters, churches, and universities all cost money; does not this fact settle the issue of priorities? In a way, it does, and in a radical way, for the reduction of all values to economic or money equivalents makes thinking about the various values and their relationships easier, if not altogether unnecessary.

A UNIVERSAL YARDSTICK

Robert Hughes asks,

> What do the soaring prices being paid for art mean? On the most obvious level, it means what everyone knows: that money is losing value. ... The culture is now getting to the point where everything that can be regarded, however distantly, as a work of art is primarily esteemed not for its ability to communicate meaning, or its use as historical evidence, or its capacity to generate aesthetic pleasure, but for its convertibility into cash.[6]

The convertibility into cash value is not confined to works of art. The rights of inheritance, alimony, palimony, and community property exemplify the translation of affectional experience into monetary equivalents. We find juries awarding money damages to unmarried lovers ousted from households and adjudicating breach of promise (not promises to marry) to share property. We need not dwell on the monetary exploitation of affectional values by show business. Sex is sold, literally, in a hundred ways from expensive drama to the crudest pornography.

The translation of civic values into economic ones is commonplace. All public service carries a price, and the service is assessed by price. Even spontaneous spurts of patriotism are not free from alert entrepreneurs who hurry to supply T-shirts, bumper stickers, flags, and souvenirs to help express patriotic fervor. And so down the line: the recreational and health values become big business. The golf tournament that does not carry a big price tag will not be covered by television because it will not serve as a profitable advertising medium. Health values are among the most costly in the budget of the ordinary citizen, and of the nation.

Education is evaluated by the amount of tuition charged directly by private colleges and indirectly in publicly financed institutions. An even more important price tag is the salary that a degree, graduate or undergraduate, commands in the marketplace. Highly paid professors must be good professors. College presidents are paid more than governors in many states. Textbook publishing business is big business. Research grants can be compared by price.

Hughes' animadversions apply not only to visual art but to all the arts. A tenor commanding $10,000 a performance is not so "good" as one commanding twice that amount and one who sings for his supper is "worth" no more. Religious values have had their money price from the beginnings of organized religion. The spectacle of Mother Theresa devoting her life to charity in India is so amazing as to be incredible; but once accorded the Nobel Prize of nearly $200,000, the religious quality was certified. Electronic evangelism is "in," and may yet be listed on the stock exchange.

Indeed, the virtues themselves acquire a price tag. Humility, for example, is recognized as a virtue, if not overdone; that is, if credible and not put on. Are there, then, grades of humility varying in genuineness and worth? There are some intriguing psychological and ethical questions here with which philosophy and literature have been concerned for centuries. Religions that value humility are especially interested in its quality, its motivation, and manifestation. Should humility be flaunted by dress, gesture, or demeanor? Or is this false humility?

These conjectures and distinctions are unnecessary if we resort to our universal yardstick. A humility that is written up in a mass media magazine, or is the centerpiece of a bestselling novel or is made into a movie is clearly superior on this yardstick than unknown humility. The humility that generates large amounts of money somewhere is good humility, so that if one is going to be humble, he should hire a good agent and become celebrated for it.

Measuring all values on an economic scale desensitizes us to the intrinsic differences in the qualities of experience and to their subtle relations. Each value domain has its distinctive quality as experienced and satisfies distinctive needs of the human personality. Each domain can enhance and inhibit the others; the art of life is to maximize and harmonize their totality. The master domain is the moral, which adjudicates conflicts between values and between high and lower ranges of value. When, therefore, the money price is the sole yardstick of value, moral adjudication of value becomes unnecessary. A $200,000 tennis tournament is equal to a $200,000 research grant is equal to a $200,000 alimony. We come to *be* what the market says we *are*—$10,000 or $15,000 or $500,000 persons—a grading already common for athletes, artists, celebrities, lawyers, doctors, and corporation executives. We sense the difference between speaking of X as a $150,000 lawyer and X as a $150,000 man or woman. And yet, this way of speaking sounds less and less odd in the 1980s.

DE-MORALIZATION

De-moralization in the narrow sense of the term consists of ignoring intentionally or inadvertently the moral issue. Re-moralizing domains of conduct that have been de-moralized requires not only knowledge about the human enterprise, which furnishes the educated mind with enlightened perspectives about life, but also virtue, the habit of making choices in accordance with moral principles. One might at this point rehearse the history of the search for the nature of virtue and its relation to reason and knowledge. Whether such a rehearsal would clarify the citizen's search for credibility is hard to say, but without some set of principles of right and wrong, good and evil, the citizen cannot re-moralize the problems of living in a democratic society. Such principles, to be functional, have to become habitual determinants of thought and feeling; and to become habits, training has to begin early, before the child can appreciate their import and justification. In a democracy such training smacks of imposition, indoctrination, and propaganda, the very opposites of rationality. That is why Dewey's CAT held out so much promise; it was a way for human beings at all but the very early ages to arrive at warranted assertions about what ought to be done in a particular situation by their free exercise of intelligence. Unfortunately, using the CAT provides us with rational ways of acting according to principles; it does not dispense with the need of having such principles.

Dewey's distinction between valuation and evaluation held out the promise that by investigating conflicting proposals for action in the light of the most tenable hypothesis as to consequences, a "consensus of uncoerced persuasion" would result. But what causes conflicts in proposals for action? In addition to differences in interests—which might be ironed out by revealing the underlying commonality—there are fundamental differences in moral principles, their validation and their role in decision.

Moral relativism or situational ethics rejects rigid adherence to principle on the ground that no moral principle is universal, which is another way of saying that the balancing of interests should be the guiding principle for group action. Aside from the theoretical difficulties of maintaining such a relativism discussed earlier, for the citizen it simply does not describe his own experience or that of his fellow citizens. They distinguish between practical compromise and moral principle. The rule in ordinary social intercourse is Don't trust unprincipled people!

MORAL RESPONSIBILITY AND CREDIBILITY

In trying to judge the credibility of information and persons, we have to rely on character traits. One of these is the willingness of the advocate of a theory or a principle to take the responsibility for its implementation. One way of evading or diminishing that responsibility is the insistence that it be judged only for what is done within a highly specialized area of competence.

The consequence, if this position is taken by all vocations, is that moral considerations will not be considered by *any* vocation. The clergy may be cited as an exception; members of the clergy are permitted and perhaps even expected to raise the moral issue, because religious doctrines usually include moral precepts. However, by sequestering religious activities to certain sites on certain days of the week (a limitation that does not apply to the electronic church), the influence on secular institutions is kept under control. Indeed, clergymen are often advised to keep their noses and sermons out of business, politics, and the morality of individual parishoners.

So it comes to pass that clients of the various professions, when unhappy with the services rendered, appeal to one of these professions for redress, namely, the law. It has been reported that even clergymen are now being sued for malpractice and, as might have been expected, lawyers themselves are not immune from such suits. Moral considerations for which the professions disclaimed responsibility are reintroduced in the name of justice. Whether they like it or not, lawyers willy-nilly are involved with morality.

Max Radin says:

> Instead of "lawful," modern lawyers are likely to use the word "right," which they stole from the moralists. This, however, is only fair retaliation, for

the word which the ancient moralists used for "right" was stolen from the lawyers. There is accordingly an association between law and morality, if only as the victims of each other's pilferings, and we have long been asked to suppose that at one time the two were identical. That may be so. However, we cannot go back so far into the authenticated history of our civilization that we can find a time when lawyer and moralist really were quite identical. The differentiation took place very early.[7]

Nevertheless, the law or the legal system of administering the law, is reluctant to abandon its formalized procedures and nice distinctions. Guilt, for example, is not the commission of an unlawful action, but what a jury, after listening to testimony presented according to rules, says a person did. "The moral logic of the system does not assume that the results of trials will always be consonant with 'truth' (an unattainable ideal), but only that trials should be conducted according to rules."[8]

The resemblance to a game is obvious, and it may well be that this is the best a human society can do, but it does make the category of justice irrelevant, for justice and injustice have to do with the "truth" about deeds and motives and consequences. And if the legal profession is not held in high esteem, it may be because human beings do not confuse a courtroom with a football field or tennis court or even a chess board.[9]

There is a question whether a social system committed to the primacy of the economic incentive can legislate justice. If there is profit in crime, there is an ever-present incentive to subvert or evade any legislation designed to prevent or punish it. The public is encouraged to do anything the law does not specifically forbid, to take advantage of any loophole. There is an economic disincentive for obeying the spirit of the law when the letter permits evading it. The equating of legality with justice by the legal establishment strengthens this disincentive.

An even more serious and practical factor working against the efforts of legislation to introduce justice is that it is caught between having to make the law cover classes of cases and the difficulty, if not impossibility, of separating the deserving from undeserving individuals who are to profit or be punished by it. If "deserving" is defined in moral terms, it is difficult to frame language that makes the distinctions functional. If, for example, the law defines indigence by a dollar amount or other physical conditions, the way is opened for the undeserving poor (and some not so poor) to subvert the intent of the law. The abuses of Medicaid and Aid to Dependent Children, which were designed to help the deserving indigent, are notorious. Because human law cannot anticipate all possible subversions of it for economic gain, there is a built-in factor that militates against justice in a society that in principle makes the economic incentive dominant.

These considerations give credence to the "utopian" argument that an investment in morality might be profitable, as was intimated in chapter 6. Not only is virtue its own reward, but conceivably it might have economic rewards as well; if the extrinsic rewards are solely economic, the virtues themselves run the danger of becoming de-moralized and degenerating into hypocrisy.

Marvin E. Wolfgang reported the results of a study of the seriousness ratings of various crimes by 60,000 individuals. The study was conducted by the Center for Studies of Criminology and Criminal Law at the University of Pennsylvania of which Professor Wolfgang is the director.

One of the findings is that the public judges white-collar crime more severely than have the courts. Illegal price fixing by some large corporations was rated as more serious than a personal robbery; environmental pollution and official corruption also received more severe ratings than might have been expected. The article concludes that "the message is that corruption has become as serious as many forms of violent and property crimes. The citizenry is saying that the victim of corruption is everybody, the body politic. Such a grave crime deserves more serious sanctions. Elected officials in the legislative, judicial, and executive branches would do well to take notice of these public perceptions."[10]

The findings prompt several observations. One is the enlarged public awareness of the effects of collective crimes, that is, crimes that involve interlocking groups and damage large groups of citizens. Inasmuch as this requires understanding of the interdependent features of modern society, the increased awareness indicates clearly a growth in the capacity for rational action by the citizenry.

But the findings also reflect the diminishing credibility of legal officialdom. The elaborate system of rules that govern courtroom maneuvers so often ends up with decisions that run counter to public morality that inevitably the legal profession is suspected of moral insensitivity, if not downright callousness. That such an elaborate system is justified ultimately by a surplus of justice over injustice has to be taken on faith, so much so that for the common man the principle itself (e.g., the presumption of innocence until formal proof of guilt is established), also comes under suspicion. The quoted paragraph holds out the hope and perhaps the expectation that the moral level of the legal establishment will rise to that of the general public.

MORALITY AND ACTION FROM PRINCIPLE

Among the most blatant examples of counter-intuitive morality are actions undertaken in the name of high moral principles. In chapter 7 some examples of doctrinaire defense of principles were cited as threats to credibility, when the advocates demanded immunity from retaliation by those who felt threatened by a particular application of their principles. Thus, for the American Civil Liberties Union to protect a Nazi or KKK organization's right to get rid of Jews, blacks, and Catholics "on principle" is *in the abstract* understandable; but that the ACLU should expect to escape the wrath of Jews, blacks, and Catholics is not.

Action from principle may raise questions not only of credibility but of morality as well. If the Nazi or KKK group does in fact carry out its program, does absolute loyalty to principle excuse the ACLU from moral responsibility for the consequences?

Alasdair MacIntyre, commenting on the debate between advocates of growth in energy production and some of the environmentalists, says: "Our evaluations should satisfy two minimal requirements of justice. The first is that everyone relevantly involved should have a chance to say what is to count as a cost and what a benefit. The second is that, so far as possible, those who receive the benefits should also be those who pay the costs and vice-versa."[11]

How often do the reform movements of the Right and Left satisfy these conditions? How often do self-appointed leaders speak for the oppressed? How often, as commentator John P. Roche put it, do crusades end up as rackets? How many reformers enjoy the luxury of self-righteousness at somebody else's expense? The antics of the radical chic and of affluent students denouncing the Vietnam war from the safety of the college campus did not lend credibility to their arguments, whatever the merits of their causes.

Under this heading may also be included conscious and unconscious parasitism. To denounce modern technology while using it is either mindlessly parasitical or hypocritical. We may not have the option of doing without a technology of which we disapprove, but to make a career of denouncing it at learned conferences in Hawaii on generous expense accounts to defray jet travel and first-class hotels and to televise these deliberations by satellite is fatal to credibility.

Acting from principle is morally admirable, and when it is in behalf of unpopular causes, often heroic. But to be morally admirable, an action must be materially as well as formally right. This means that adherence to a principle should not create injustice by its foreseeable consequences. A now notorious example is the *Bakke* case in which a student, who by no stretch of imagination or logic was responsible for the race discrimination against blacks, was called upon to atone for it by giving up his right to admission to a California medical school. That discrimination is bad in general does not mean that injustice in particular is good, and to make an innocent individual suffer for a collective crime in which he had no part is not just. The body politic in its contrition could tax itself in order to establish more medical schools, and the credibility of affluent intellectuals who argued against Bakke "on principle" would be enhanced if they were ready to share in Bakke's atonement. Militant proponents of affirmative action would increase their moral credibility if they resigned their places in schools, business, and government in favor of those whose cause they are promoting.

Similarly, the defenders of terrorism in behalf of "holy" causes would be more credible if they were ready to recompense the victims, who are almost never guilty of the evils the terrorists are trying to eradicate. We can resist the fanatic injustice of terrorism only by a commitment to justice as an unqualified right of the individual person. Otherwise terrorism will be justified as necessary counterviolence against the group that opposes the holy cause, regardless of the guilt or innocence of its victims. It becomes "a necessary form of social and moral regeneration." As Fanon says, "Violence, violence committed by the people, violence organized and educated by its leaders, make it possible for the masses to understand social truths and gives the key to them."[12]

The respect for principle is not the same as self-righteous idolatry of it. It is one thing to say: "I shall be true to my principle, no matter what it does to *me*"; it is quite another to say: "I shall be true to my principle, no matter what it does to others." The "others" may be innocent victims.

The responsibility test does not determine the validity or value of the principles involved, just as it does not determine propositional truth. As long as the principle remains at the level of abstract argument, no test of credibility is needed. But when commitment to principle impinges on the lives of people and creates innocent victims, the credibility test becomes imperative. The strongest argument for the primacy of principle is that to limit it would conduce to greater evil than applying it without exception. Even here it must be shown that no circumstances would make the application of the principle unjust to innocent individuals. Unfortunately, we are unable to define a principle precisely and yet not fritter it away in definitional subtleties. Nor are we wise enough to foresee and forestall the efforts to abuse it.

The rejection of the posture that a principle must be upheld at any cost is not the same as the rejection of the principle. One might hold that freedom of speech is an absolute good and yet insist that defending it entails sharing the cost of its unjust consequences. Conversely, staunch advocates of the absolute primacy of free speech often justify it on the ground that there are no absolute truths and therefore all should be free to say what they like.

Of all the principles that people who act from principle worship, the right of free speech is perhaps the most sacrosanct. Not only is freedom in general an intrinsic good, but without this one, a democratic free society would be hard to envisage. It is understandable, therefore, that those who act from this principle will be moved to defend it regardless of what is uttered and the consequences of its utterance.

I do not propose to argue the familiar but difficult distinctions between utterance and incitement. These are partly matters of law and get easily lost in its mazes. However, there is a credibility criterion that can be applied to those who act from principle at all costs. The criterion is sincerity and authenticity, and the tests for these are willingness to suffer *personally* the consequences of the principle being put into practice. That the defender of free speech is willing to have others suffer the consequences goes without saying.

A reporter who goes to jail rather than betray a source has more credibility as a defender of free speech than the professor who calls for someone else to preach revolution. That so many ardent defenders of free speech are in a position to evade its consequences deprives the stance of much of its moral significance. Great causes and great principles, like great religions, rely heavily on the blood of their martyrs.

CREDIBILITY AND SACRIFICE

When an official in any organization demands sacrifice from the workers or from the citizenry in the name of the common good, truth and credibility questions arise. Is the need for the sacrifice as the official describes it? Would the sacrifices he demands really promote the common good? These are truth questions and perhaps can be settled by empirical evidence combined with a consensus on some goal or other. For example, it may be the case that in order for the schools to stay open in a city, 1000 teachers will have to be eliminated from the payroll. It may not be the case, however, and it may be that such a measure is not the most likely one to keep the schools open. For example, if there is a teacher strike, the schools will not remain open.

Even if the claim of the official is factually correct, it is morally unsatisfying. For it would not be out of place for each of the 1000 teachers slated for firing to ask: Why me? Why not other teachers or supervisors or administrators? One might argue that a collective good requires a collective sacrifice, not arbitrarily selected individual ones. Inequality of *benefits*, as has been noted, can be justified if it contributes to the greater good of the greatest number and if it benefits the least advantaged. Inequality of *sacrifice* is harder to justify on this principle, especially if the sacrifice is imposed rather than freely chosen by the individual. We recognize, for example, the heroism of David taking on Goliath for the sake of the people, and we gratefully accept the martyrdom of individuals for the benefit of the group. This inequality is freely chosen, and that is why it qualifies as moral heroism. The imposition of such a role even by custom, as in the sacrifice of human beings in rituals, or the drafting of men to die for their country, deprives the sacrifice of its heroism and converts it into an implacable necessity, one that becomes more and more difficult to understand and justify in civilized societies.

The unseemliness of Congress asking the citizens to sacrifice their standard of living while congressmen retain their salaries and perquisites is a clue to their loss of credibility. And that so many of them seem not to sense it amazes the citizen even more.

REFERENCES

1. International Symposium on Science, Technology, and the Human Prospect, April 1979; A Report of the Edison Electric Institute, Symposium Supplement to the *New York Review of Books*, p. 2.

2. Ibid., pp. 5–6.

3. Ibid., p. 11

4. Ibid., p. 7.

5. Ibid., p. 9.

6. Robert Hughes, *Time*, 31 December 1979.

7. Max Radin, "The Permanent Problems of the Law," in *Jurisprudence in Action : An Anthology of Legal Essays*, pp. 416–17.

8. Graham Hughes commenting on Robert Reiff, *The Invisible Victim* in the *New York Review of Books* 27 (6 March 1980), p. 3.

9. A Louis Harris survey of public confidence in 17 institutions showed that law firms were tied for 16th place with labor, above advertising agencies but well below medicine, television news, and Congress.

In the *New York Times* (10 February 1980) Linda Greenhouse, reporting on the efforts of the American Bar Association commission to draft new rules of professional conduct, says: "Whether time is in fact running out on law as a self-regulating profession, the current code's failure to address—or in some cases even to acknowledge—the toughest dilemmas of modern law practice has clearly not made these dilemmas go away."

10. *New York Sunday Times*, 2 March 1980.

11. *New York Review of Books*, Symposium Supplement, p. 9.

12. Franz Fannon, *Les Damnés de la Terre* (Paris, 1961). For a good discussion of terrorism, *see* Paul Johnson, *The Enemies of Society*, New York: Atheneum 1977, chap. 19.

9

The Re-Moralization of Truth

The remedy for de-moralization is re-moralization. The remedy for the
arbitrary narrowing of relevance is to broaden the contexts of our problems so that their ramifications in the various value domains are discovered. The remedy for irresponsibility, hidden agenda, dissembling, and
evasion is awareness and disclosure, not only of facts but of motives as
well. The criteria of credibility are purity of heart, sincerity, authenticity,
and commitment. These terms signal a shift into discourse of a different
key, the discourse of morality and character, and bring one closer to the
dangers of sermonizing. It also marks a shift from propositional to existential truth, the stuff out of which sermons are made, but which sermons do not exhaust.

Truth turns existential when the nature and value of persons, the
reality of norms, ideals, and freedom come under scrutiny. Existential
truth can be hazardous because it removes assertions about the human
reality from the constraints of logic and science; for this reason, if no
other, it should be the last resort rather than the first when we are trying
to adjudicate conflicting truth claims. Existential questions are the stuff
of theology, philosophy, history, art, and literature. Human beings carry
around strong convictions on these matters, but they are not truths for
which there is proof or verification in the ordinary sense of these terms.
Over these ideas always hovers the possibility that they are man-made
illusions diverting us from the reality of rocks and rivers, bones and flesh.

The Danish philosopher Søren Kierkegaard in the nineteenth century argued that in matters of the Christian dogma, subjectivity was the truth, especially the fundamental one that God became man in order to atone for the latter's sins. Such a doctrine, Kierkegaard held, was rationally absurd. If it were to be grasped at all, it would be in complete commitment to a desperate gamble that it was true.

That certain spiritual dogmas could be known only by faith was not a thesis original with Kierkegaard. He did, however, bring out with dramatic clarity the need for an epistemological scrutiny of faith. How does it achieve its probative value if deprived of the criteria employed in ordinary knowing? The probative power of faith, according to Kierkegaard, lies in the credibility of the witness, and this is established when the witness is willing to live in the truth he proclaims; so witnessed, it becomes existential truth. But is existential truth confined to the dogmas of religion? Are there more mundane assertions, the truth of which is scientifically doubtful and perhaps indeterminable but in which one is called upon to live?

Bertrand Russell observed that the more rigorous the demands for logical proof, the less we can prove and the more we have to act on faith or retreat to an unlivable skepticism. In short, many of our most important beliefs cannot meet logical demands for proof or the empirical requirements for evidence. How, then, do we test these articles of faith?

TRUTH AS SUBJECTIVITY

The most dramatic and extreme form of verification by the act of a witness is martyrdom. Thus Justin Martyr (c. A.D. 100–160) said that the courage of the executed Christians convinced him of their divine inspiration.

> It is clear that no one can terrify or subdue us who believe in Jesus Christ, throughout the whole world. For it is clear that though beheaded, and crucified, and thrown to wild beasts, in chains, in fire, and all other kinds of torture, we do not give up our confession; but the more such things happen, the more do others, in larger numbers, become believers.[1]

The rationalist would retort that no number of martyrs could establish the truth or falsity of the doctrine of the Resurrection, but the willingness to die for the belief established beyond doubt that the believer was sincere in his faith. To live in one's faith may mean dying for it.

Kierkegaard argued that in the religious sphere subjectivity is the truth. But clearly subjectivity in the ordinary meaning of knowledge is *not* the truth. The truth relation implies some kind of correspondence between an assertion and its referent, but what if the referent is a state of consciousness? Then the assertion refers to the property of a subject, a conclusion that rejects the positivistic demand that in a truth relation the referent be a publicly observable object independent of the subject. If the reality to which an assertion refers is a subjective state of a self, it is not open to public scrutiny for verifying the assertions about it. The way to verify them, Kierkegaard argues, is by being a witness of the truth being asserted; living as if one's life depended on its being true.[2]

Among the items in the existential truth basket are such entities as selves, ideals, values, and moral principles for judging values. Surely these are real, if real means persisting through time, retaining some sort of identifiable structure, and, above all, having demonstrable influence on human thought and action.

The most important entities that must be classified as existential are selves. Selves act, feel, and think. Selves formulate the rules for verification by which they rule themselves and everything else in or out of existence. Science can do relatively little with selves; almost nobody can recognize themselves or any other selves in the descriptions of them given by psychologists. The more imaginative accounts by psychoanalysts and novelists are more interesting reading. Sigmund Freud reduced the lofty claims of human ideals to sublimations undertaken to conceal or atone for the raw instinctual drives of sex and aggression. Nothing testifies better to the uniqueness of human consciousness than its efforts to reduce mind to simple reflexes and its strivings to physiological deprivations: to prove that civilization was a mistake. It would never occur to beasts or angels to try to do so.[3]

Simulated intelligence comes excitingly close to closing the gap between consciousness and molecules, but never quite makes it—the reduction of thought to the switching on and off of an electric current does not quite do it. One electric impulse can activate another and another and another; but when all is switched, an electric twitch is not a thought, not even when that electric twitch is demonstrably occurring in the cells of a brain.

Sublimation is the pivotal and critical concept in the description of the human reality. Sublimation is a function of the imagination that transforms lust into love; feeding into dining; death into heroism. Is sublimation the key to the human essense, or is it a lie? Which is more human—lust or love; feeding or dining; chemistry or poetry? Does it make sense to ask which is more real?

Imagination is the creator of possibility, a necessary condition for the *human* actuality. Without imagination generating a realm of what *might* be, there would be no ground for freedom, choice, norms, and morality itself. The emergence of conceptual reasoning curbed some of imagination's wildness, but sensory images of feeling could well have been our earliest awareness of the world. The threatening sky and smiling sun were imagic reports of how matters stood between men and nature—an ontological meteorology, so to speak.

Because feelings of the self about itself and about the natural world can be objectified in images, the arts present us with images of human import that, as Wordsworth put it, can be recollected in tranquillity. And so recollected, they convert the inner subjective reality into an object of contemplation. In this sense we can speak of art as yielding feelingful knowledge and knowledgeful feeling, the synthesis of fact and value. However, the feeling portrayed is not identical with the feeling as actually undergone, while the knowledge is not propositional truth about feeling—it is not psychology. These images of feeling could well have been the sensory nuclei of concepts, and that is why scholars are drawn to them as the primordial source of meaning. The hermeneutics of myth, ritual, and ceremony is a kind of cultural archeology—a dig to unearth the feelings and beliefs objectified and congealed in linguistic and artistic structures.[4]

No doubt this is a good place to dig. If propositional and existential truth have a common origin, it may be found in the human play with images and words. As with other scholarly enthusiasms, the search for the sources of the human reality and its subsequent development by removing overlying strata of meaning can become a pretext for playing interesting intellectual games. There is a place for intellectual play—the academy—and inventing scholarly games is good intellectual exercise for professors and Ph.D candidates. This is not said to denigrate academics, because the play of ideas is the motor of all intellectual creativity; but from the point of view of the citizen, who is not a scholar, the game is not the reality, just as an athletic contest is not mistaken for a real-life contest, despite the seriousness with which it is played. Conventions such as picture frames and concert halls warn us not to take the "message" of art literally, but such warning signals are not always posted by the scholars to apprise the laity that they are playing a game, albeit with utmost seriousness.

Examples are not hard to find. Much of the linguistic and logical analysis that characterizes formal scholarship in philosophy substitutes discourse about the logical properties of philosophical discourse for concern with substantive philosophical issues. Fine-spun and sophisticated articles argue on how to talk properly about God, freedom, and immortality, or whether it is proper to talk about them at all. Much of the work in formal aesthetics, for example, is concerned with the necessary and sufficient logical and linguistic conditions for making statements about aesthetic values rather than with works of art. In literature and literary criticism, one commentator has remarked that the nature of criticism becomes more important than the work being evaluated.[5] Academic scholarship takes to such substitution naturally, because it is by nature reflective about itself, and language as such has no natural limitation to reflexivity and iteration. Substantive issues become more and more attenuated into procedures and procedures about the study of procedures. And at each new level, a new field of specialization is created, and with luck and money, a new academic department comes into being.

Just as the meaning and reality of selves elude the efforts to transform them into objects for empirical inquiry and generalization, so does the meaning and reality of the idea and ideal of the good society. The ploys for deriving a general will or general good over and above the goods of individuals are familiar, interesting, and, by and large, not convincing because morality and self-interest are not identical. If men are no more than clever, greedy, and brutal animals, then no scheme for the common good will deter some of the more clever ones from finding ways of subverting it for their private good. Hypothesizing a state of nature in which reasonable men would choose to associate for the common good underestimates the number and astuteness of men who will use their reason to anticipate and subvert what the reasonable men would do.

We are not born with the ideal of a common good. We are born into some kind of society, to be sure, but not into an ideal one. We soon learn the value of filial affection, and by imagination these feelings are exfoliated into the ideal of a brotherhood of man living in a universal family. This ideal, or similar ones, becomes more than a figment of the imagination when it captures the imagination of enough individuals and persuades them to live as if it were a cosmic command. A corrupt society resists capture by such ideals of the imagination.

Perhaps enough has been said to show that the contents of subjective or existential reality are far more varied than religious experience. By enlarging the stock of propositional truth, science has not diminished the scope of existential truth; on the contrary, it has created an ever increasing number of existential problems, the problems of credibility.

ARE EXISTENTIAL TRUTHS RELIABLE?

The distinction between empirical truths about objects and existential truths about selves and their creations is easier to draw than to use. Empirical truth does not ensure its credibility; existential truth does not guarantee its own reliability. Granted that the existential truth is uttered by a sincere, authentic self, ready to be a witness, how do we know that the speaker is not demented, suffering from hallucinations, or a fanatic so intoxicated with a vision of the world that he is ready to become a martyr in its defence? For there is no limit to the ideas and impulses for which the fanatic is willing to risk or pledge his life. There is no crime, no violence, no inhumanity that has not been justified as an existential truth worthy of the extreme sacrifice. How can we spot the fanatic, the fake, and the sadly misguided apostles of existential truth?[6]

One important species of fanatic is the charismatic leader. According to Max Weber, such a leader derives his legitimacy from an accepted relation to supernatural power and the ability to produce the results promised to the followership. How this is done is less important than that it is done, so that the leader can be trusted for the future. The charismatic leader acquires credibility also by not working for economic gain; he is not a rational schemer for advantage to himself. But the holder of charisma may give it up or the connection with the supernatural may be broken; the leader is rejected by his leader.[7]

The criteria of existential truth must be sought within the nature of the self. Are there properties or structures that constitute it and limit what it can and ought to do? Is there a human nature, such that some behavior can be ruled out as nonhuman or inhuman? And what is the import of the word "humane," if it differs from "human?" To these questions scholars give the full range of answers. Some think this nature is a fixed structure given at birth to all humankind; others deny any fixed human nature, yet would wish to exclude behavior such as wanton cruelty from the meaning of "human." Some believe human nature to be determined by the genes; others explain it by social learning of the "mores," which are introjected so that in time they seem to have originated within the individual and to be as natural as having two eyes or two hands. Having one eye or three hands, incest, cannibalism, and infanticide would all be classified as "unnatural."

Even if this controversy were resolvable, I shall not try to do so. It may be sufficient to speculate that through natural selection certain variations in human attitudes towards life acquired survival value and became norms of the species. That these attitudes may lose their survival value at some stage in human history need not be ruled out, but that some have survived because of their social value need not be denied either. Credibility is on the side of those who argue for a stable (not immutable) set of norms that define humanity, rather than on the side of those who deny it only because it is conceivable that the contrary might be true. That of which the contrary or even a plausible alternative may be imagined is not necessarily or even probably false. Existential truth does not claim to be either a logical truth following inexorably from indubitable premises, or an empirical generalization supported by indubitable instances. Existentially, the question "Is there a human nature?" is a question about the conception of life that does justice to the ideals human imagination and thought have created. Can such a conception command the willingness to live as if it were true? Can we live with a concept of human nature that leaves the way open to every possibility and excludes nothing as nonhuman or inhuman?

Inherent or acquired, the category of the human includes that of rationality, and rationality is an ordering faculty of the mind. It imposes order on feeling, imagination, and on itself. The intelligible is the orderly; content without form is unintelligible and perhaps not even perceptible. The fanatic distorts the limiting governance of reason, of logic, and of evidence; and when he does order his thinking, it is by a highly idiosyncratic logic. The fanatic insists on the consistency of his fantasies, and other human beings can at times sense the consistency while denying its sense.[8] Even the most fanatic charismatic leader finds it imperative to "explain" his failures, if not his successes. The self cannot refuse the test of rationality, although it may do weird things to meet it. Therefore it does no violence to selfhood and existential reality to deny it complete freedom from the constraints of rationality. Selfhood is not a charter for irrationality.

The self is limited in another way. For Kant, the experience of moral obligation presupposed an ability to choose, contrary to its desires. Only a law that binds all human wills would justify such constraints on individual wishes. To be consistent with free choice, such a law would therefore be legislated by each self for itself. "There is therefore but one categorical imperative, namely this: *Act only on that maxim whereby thou canst at the same time will that it should become a universal law.*"[9]

It is this possibility that limits man's inclinations to pleasures of both the flesh and the imagination. It is also what gives to the human self the ultimate dignity—and yields what Kant calls the practical imperative. "So act as to treat humanity, whether in thine own person or in that of any other, in every case as an end withal, never as a means only."[10]

In addition to the legitimate controls over imagination exercised by logic and science, the ignoring of which can produce untold misery, there is the Kantian test of impartiality, viz., willingness to have the maxim of one's conduct become a universal law. This goes a step beyond credibility, the willingness of the fanatic to live by the "truth" he proclaims, but neither impartiality nor credibility are sufficient to protect us from fanaticism. Hitler, for example, could pass these tests. The further question, therefore, is whether the doctrine or way of life being propounded is consistent with the Kantian imperative to treat selves as ends and never as means only. If there is an ultimate existential truth, this would be a prime candidate for the title.

PRINCIPLES OF UNITY

Having urged the distinction between existential truth and propositional truth; between the reality of objects and that of subjects, it now becomes necessary to build some sort of bridge between them. The human self is at all times a unified entity in which bodily and psychological processes are going on together, and the fact that we can distinguish them *in mente* does not mean that we have any convincing examples of their existing separately. At this point the citizen might well ask the point of distinguishing what in any event cannot be separated?

One point is that there would be no philosophy if such distinctions were not made, and indeed all efforts to carry on conceptual thinking would be impossible without drawing boundaries around the meaning of concepts. One cannot think and talk about everything at the same time. Philosophy is noted for its preoccupation with persistent problems. The mechanism for devising a persistent problem is to pick two concepts the meanings of which exclude each other by definition and yet which are inseparable in existence. Mind and body, the one and the many, appearance and reality, fact and value are samples of dichotomies that have provided philosophers with persistent problems. The occupational survival of philosophy depends on finding or inventing problems that other philosophers can neither solve nor abandon. Much of the philosophical literature turned out in the last twenty centuries in the Western world consists of claims to have solved one of these puzzles and counterattacks showing that the attempt was a failure. The great names in the history of philosophy are the problem inventors. Plato and Zeno are among the most notable.

> Since the time of Kant, it has become more and more apparent to non-philosophers that a really professional philosopher can supply [*or destroy*] a philosophical foundation for just about anything. This is one reason why philosophers have, in the course of our century, become increasingly isolated from the rest of culture. Our proposals to guarantee this and clarify that have come to strike our fellow intellectuals as merely comic.[11]

Human action transforms these philosophical problems into existential predicaments. Willy-nilly such action brings together mind and body, the one and the many, fact and value, the particular and the universal. Thus action itself is a demand for unification of existential and propositional truth, and especially when the aim is to act rationally.

The scientific enterprise devoted to warranted assertion is itself a moral enterprise. The process of inquiry and its rules of evidence are themselves "oughts" to which the scientist is committed. Not to fudge the evidence, not to allow "nonscientific" considerations to influence the conclusions, not to lie about procedures, and the like, are all moral injunctions to intellectual *action*. The credibility of science depends on its commitment to these values.

The code of ethics of a profession is also a unifier of fact and value, propositional and existential truth. To be sure, the code tries to limit the interest of the client to a narrow area (e.g., bodily health or protection against misuse of legal procedures). Some items in the code protect the client from the use of professional skill *merely* to benefit the non-professional interests of the practitioner. However, as soon as the welfare of the client is introduced, the sharp boundaries between professional and nonprofessional interests are made fuzzy. Mental anguish gets mixed up with physical pain, the duty to preserve life with the desire of the patient to end it.

Institutions and membership in them are also unifying forces of the self, a fact that surfaces when an institution such as a household begins to disintegrate.

A direct result of the disintegration of the household is the division of sexuality from fertility and their virtual takeover by specialists. The specialists of sexuality are the sexual clinicians and the pornographers, both of whom subsists on the increasing possibility of sex between people who neither need nor care about each other. The specialists of human fertility are the evangelists, technicians, and salesmen of birth control, who subsist upon our failure to see any purpose in sexual discipline.[12]

But just as science has its morals, so morality has its logic. Consistency is an imperative in moral affairs as well as in theoretical ones. The willingness to have an action apply to oneself, which has been cited many times as evidence for credibility, is a form of consistency.

The de-moralization of truth, therefore, is not the result of a metaphysical or ontological chasm between knowledge and character, fact and value. It is a deliberate exploitation of their separability in thought and discourse. This separation is necessary and justifiable for conceptual clarity and logical precision, but its elevation into a professional strategy to evade responsibility is not.

The real world is more like a restless lava flow than a chessboard with pieces moving according to predetermined rules. The flow may be interrupted by our separations and distinctions, but it flows around them and resumes its undifferentiated progress. Our tallest fences between disciplines and professional concerns are vulnerable to the recombinations mandated by the dialectic of modern life.* Engineers, for example, build bridges, dams, turbines, and what not, yet every public building or project is subject to political and economic considerations that go beyond the sheer technical requirements of traditional engineering schools. The environmental concerns of the last decade are wholesome enough and make sense, but one group's whales are another group's employment. Today's lawyers are pulled into consumer group actions, the sex habits of litigious clients, and a host of claims for all sorts of human rights and privileges.

The professionals who have prided themselves on their specializations, on their ability to cut the web of relevance so that they can operate within their own rules, are now forced to expand their interests and their

---

*As a weird example of this dialectic, consider a strange effect of the oil crisis. We are familiar with the effect on the American automobile industry, the vacation habits of Americans, and the like, but how is one to explain the increased profits of a tire company in one of its departments during these critical times? One such company reported that the sale of rubber heels had greatly increased in recent years because people walked more and had their shoes repaired more frequently. Of course, the rise in the price of new shoes may also have contributed to the prosperity of the shoe repair industry.

rules. Law schools employ sociologists, economists, and environmentalists. Engineering schools have had to become familiar with the methods of the social sciences, especially as they are employed in the shaping and evaluation of governmental policies. Schools of medicine are offering courses in ethics.

These tendencies and developments strain the clear-cut divisions on the campus of the university. Disciplines nudge each other as new technologies call in the resources of many forms of inquiry. The data processing industry and the use of computers in general have brought together disciplines and technologies into new clusters. Recombinant DNA research is an example of disciplines coming together and opening new technological possibilities. So is space technology. One can expect the efforts of the United States to develop synthetic fuels to have the same sort of mixing effect on academic, professional, and institutional life.

The alternation of specialization with its de-moralization and reintegration necessitated by new social demands sets up swings between pessimism and optimism. It holds out the hope that what is frustrating today may be reinforcing and supportive a few years hence, and vice versa. All of which complicate attempts to characterize the mood of the country at any time because so much depends in which phase of the alternation individuals and groups happen to be.

Pessimism tends to rise when good and evil seem to be randomized in their incidence, and when institutions, professions, and value schemata seem highly specialized and differentiated. This has been referred to as de-moralization. In this stage the remarkable advances in technology seem to increase rather than decrease frustrations.

Optimism is grounded in the reintegrative phases of the culture when new fields are opened that require the breakdown of old specializations. At such times new technology promises a victory over frustration. Science fiction and more sober speculation are intimating the possibility of the supertechnology—lasers, recombinant DNA, interplanetary travel, and the hormonal equivalent of the fountains of youth. This prospect keeps our society traveling in the direction that all genuinely human societies must travel. It is the idealizing, creative imaginative stretching the limits of human achievement. Without a high level of creativity, a society can at best hope for a peaceful truce with nature and time; a hope that nature will be sufficiently benign to sustain its members in ways that up to now have had survival value. Without this stretching of possibility, the status quo may be too readily accepted as irremediable.

Supertechnology is not the only option. Intelligent austerity might be another. At the risk of moralizing, consider the suggestion that a modicum of austerity might be not only a social virtue but also economically productive. In a dynamic capitalistic economy, austerity borders on economic sin. To lose faith in ever accelerating consumption is economic blasphemy. Yet the waste in our society is an embarassment at home and at every international conference.

The citizen, whether familiar or not with the mysteries of international trade and finance, with the distribution of mineral resources and the relative potentials for agricultural production—and for the most part he is not—can see all around him the abuse of a bountiful culture. Showing dogs and cats endorsing their favorite foods on the same television program that portrays infants with swollen bellies in some regions of Africa or Asia is a cause for embarrassment, even though we are told that the foods prepared for pets could not be used to relieve hunger here or abroad. Miracle technology may, of course, let us have an unlimited number of pets and no swollen bellies.

Our efforts at recycling have shown the extent of waste in glass, paper, and metals. Our overflowing garbage cans provide further argument for austerity in demand, supply-side economics notwithstanding. Why should not the productivity index subtract waste from production? There is a moral and political issue here, of course, because the pet food industry, the bottle-making industry, and other manufacturers of potential waste provide jobs for workers so that they too can earn enough to waste on their own account. Perhaps the manpower needed to correct the effects of waste might provide enough jobs to replace those devoted to producing it.

A decent, intelligent, honest austerity, moreover, is a virtue that the individual can practice without involving himself in large and complicated social efforts. It can be part of a design for personal living. It encourages reflection on what is really necessary and what is merely desirable or fashionable. Austerity is a hard virtue to counsel in a culture that has convinced its citizenry that the truly American way is to use credit to spend two or three times one's income; that to create demand is as important as meeting it; that the faster a product becomes obsolescent, the better the market for new products, the better for America.

It is not surprising that citizens brought up on the virtues of maximizing expenditures should be puzzled when its most vociferous advocates decry federal spending. If waste and profligacy are good in private consumption, why does it become bad when the government indulges in it? After all, a ten-dollar bill spent for groceries or liquor by a relief recipient or a bureaucrat has the same value in the economy as the same amount spent by an advertising executive. Neither amount was payment for the physical production of goods that can be consumed by human beings. If buying power is the criterion for the economic value of an activity, the relief recipient is relatively way ahead of the advertising executive. The relief recipient is 100 percent buying power.

An achieving, dynamic, impatient society pays a price for the heady pleasure of progress. The mechanism for social justice, for keeping the competition fair, cannot keep up with the inventiveness of those who can profit from injustice. We have not solved the conflict between progress and injustice. The capacity of the system to create misery and failure still outruns its ability to alleviate them. Our own society has made valiant efforts to institutionalize compassion for the casualties of the system, but human compassion is limited. It operates in a relatively narrow circle, and those who can do so, move away from concentrations of misery rather than enlarge the circle of their sympathy.

THE MAKING OF A SELF

There comes a time when the citizen can run no farther from his world or himself, and he must ask anew the kind of self he can become and honestly maintain in a modern, complex, interdependent civilization. This is the moment of existential truth, when the Kantian imperative poses the question. What kind of action and character would I legislate for myself, if what I choose were to become a universal law—for all men? And would I live by that law, come what may? This is moralism with a vengeance, but the proper question is whether these questions can be evaded. If credibility depends on traits of character, then the credibility questions that have been raised in so many aspects of life cannot be answered without some venture into existential truth, that is, into the character of those who make ostensibly warranted assertions about social policy and action.

It is easy to slip from accenting the importance of self into celebrating selfishness. Some of the liberation movements of the last decade have been accused of doing so. Such expressions as "How do I feel?" "This isn't me," and "I want to get in touch with my feelings" have prompted the tags "the me generation" and narcissism. Such celebration of self-centeredness might be called moral solipsism or moral hedonism. Questions might be raised whether such a view of life can be defended. Is it a position that one could will as a universal law? Does it take into account the moral claims of other selves? Conceivably, one might argue that most private acts have no harmful consequences for others and that hurting others would not be something an individual would be "comfortable with" and it "wouldn't be me." How do we deal with someone who is "comfortable with" hurting others?

Conceivability is not credibility. To be credible the narcissist should be able to live as if he believed that it is right for him to ignore the sentiments and judgment of his fellows. Perhaps some can, but the insistence of many free spirits that their fellows accept them without criticism or resentment betokens a need for social approval that in principle the sincere and authentic narcissist should be able to live without. It is an admission that "right" implies a principle that transcends particular desires of particular individuals. To be a self existentially is to be a citizen in a *kingdom* of ends, a society of selves. Wishes, impulses, desires are not self-legitimating in such a society.

Nor is conscience a sufficient guide to choosing the self one is committed to become. Conscience, psychologists say, is the introjection of the societal demands made upon us, and while conscience is a reliable reminder that an action or failure to act is morally out of kilter, as a guide to what ought to be done it is not always helpful.

MORAL KNOWLEDGE

Knowledge of some kind is needed to correct the intuitive dictates of conscience, on the one hand, and the prompting of affective urges, on the other. But what kind of knowledge?

For example, what happens if we violate the traffic laws? We are expected to know the consequences; ignorance of the law is no excuse, the law says. We are expected to know how machinery, railroads, airplanes, automobiles, and electrical appliances work before we use them in order to avoid harming others. Inasmuch as a great deal of misery is caused by ignorance of the way things work, this kind of knowledge is a necessary ingredient of moral knowledge. It helps us implement our good intentions by producing consequences that meet the moral claims of others as we intended they should.

More directly related to moral knowledge is what at first blush seems foreign to it, namely, the mores of the community and of the culture. Sumner, it seems to me, did not exaggerate the moral force and relevance of the mores. They were the result of certain folkways and usages being perceived as related to the good of the group, the public good.[13] The mores are the short-hand, encapsulated moral generalizations of a culture that are learned informally and reinforced by the community. It is knowledge of and respect for the mores that most citizens have in mind when they urge the schools to undertake moral education. Training in the automatic respect for the mores is a more accurate description of their expectations; automatic respect is a far more reliable control on the behavior of the young than ethical disputation. Whether the mores will withstand the scrutiny of ethical reflection is another matter; but one can be sure that in the community, disregard of the mores will not be taken kindly. Not to understand this is not only a mark of social ineptness, but also of a lack of what might be called moral intelligence.

When Socrates enunciated the enigmatic and challenging doctrine that virtue is knowledge, he must have had in mind knowledge that goes beyond prudence and etiquette. For in spite of such prudential knowledge, some of us smoke too much, eat too much, and yield to temptations fully aware that we shall regret having done so. How, then, could Socrates say that no man chooses evil knowingly; that evil choices are the result of ignorance?

If there is a kind of knowledge that *automatically* produces commitment, then there is no conflict between knowing and willing. It blocks out all contrary desires. Plato hinted at this kind of knowledge in the *Repub-*

lic. It would crown the Guardians' training in mathematics and self-control; when they would rise above discursive thinking about hypotheses and get a glimpse of the eternal forms of goodness, truth, and beauty. The language of Plato at that point resembles that of religious conversion, a literal turning around so that everything is seen in a new light and perspective. Once achieved, this vision would produce so strong a desire to embody these forms that evil would not have a chance.

> If this is true, we must conclude that education is not what it is said to be by some, who profess to put knowledge into a soul which does not possess it, as if they could put sight into blind eyes. On the contrary, our own account signifies that the soul of every man does possess the power of learning the truth and the organ to see it with; and that, just as one might have to turn the whole body round in order that the eye should see the light instead of darkness, so the entire soul must be turned away from this changing world, until its eye can bear to contemplate reality and that supreme splendour which we called the Good. Hence there may well be an art whose aim would be to effect this very thing, the conversion of the soul, in the readiest way; not to put the power of sight into the soul's eye, which already has it, but to ensure that, instead of looking in the wrong direction, it is turned the way it ought to be.[14]

Given such a knowledge, we could, as did Socrates, criticize the mores of our time, carry on disputations about virtue with young men, and be invited to drink the hemlock for "corrupting" them. And, one might add, given this divine knowledge, one might, as did Socrates, have no fear of death, let alone the disapproval of his fellow citizens. To the citizen, such pronouncements are inspiring, and sages like Socrates have a high credibility, especially if they have taken hemlock to prove their sincerity and willingness to live and die by their principles. But how does one become an everyday Socrates?

There are a number of prescriptions. One is to be "born again" in the religious sense; to achieve a new awareness of a religious doctrine and to have one's life profoundly altered thereby. The new awareness presumably provides the kind of knowledge that qualifies as virtue and possibly salvation as well. Like the Platonic conversion, it unites will, desire, and action. The community of believers are sorry for those who have not been reborn.

Another ploy is to leave the complex civilization for a more simple and purer one, an echo of Rousseau's formula for regeneration of self and society. And still another is a holy revolution in which one joins others who are willing to risk everything to save the world. A safer version of saving the world is to join reform movements of one kind or another. The ideology of the movement is also the kind of knowledge that guarantees virtue.

But why, the citizen might ask, should the knowledge required for the formation of the self, for the moral self, be so dramatic, so soaked in tension and crisis? Why a special revelation? Why should not the various ingredients of virtue be acquired informally, almost routinely, in the life of the community and more formally in school? In a democratic society, does not education for an enlightened citizenry include existential as well as propositional truth?

This question misses the point that the Socratic doctrine is making, namely, that the ordinary knowledge of the mores and codes of respectability are pale and poor substitutes for the insight and certainty of the dialectical revelation. Social anxiety and twinges of conscience, in this view, are only symptoms of our ignorance of what is *really* the goal and reward of human life. Schools and ordinary community life are not suitable agencies for the kind of knowledge that is virtue. Plato places the stage of dialectic above the ordinary curriculum and even above good instruction in mathematics. Even the more modest and pedestrian efforts at "moral education" depend on a congruity between school and community, a congruity that cannot be taken for granted in a society as large and diversified as ours.

There was a time when the American public school was expected to have a part in this existential enlightenment. The religious homogeneity of the community provided education for virtue informally. The middle-class WASP mores shaped the norms for citizen behavior in all departments of life. The tides of immigrants were expected to assimilate both the ethos of democracy and the WASP mores, including a respect for schooling, hard work, competition, self-reliance.

Whatever the historical revisionists say, it is hard to believe that many of those early immigrants did not assimilate these values and codes of conduct. They constitute the core of the middle class today. And it is equally clear that the assumptions of the melting pot on which the public school operated until the middle of the twentieth century are now questioned in some quarters and rejected in others. There is no dominant view of the democratic ethos and the public good. The erstwhile faith that reasonable human beings by concerted thought could arrive at a common good has been disrupted by the thesis that each individual can and should define his or her good, and that this takes precedence over every other determination of the good. In short, there is no public good that the public school can be said to serve. Deprived of its implicit mission, it is assigned as many missions as there are groups vocal enough to make their demands known and heard, and whatever influence it may have on morality is virtually destroyed.

This brings the problem back to Dewey's formulation of it. Can formal schooling so use the method of intelligence that the citizenry can unite warranted assertion of theory with warranted commitments to belief?

REFERENCES

1. For an account of martyrdom and the diverse attitudes toward it, see Elaine Pagels, "The Defeat of the Gnostics," *New York Review of Books* 36, no. 19 (6 December 1979): 43–51.

2. Søren Kierkegaard's *Concluding Unscientific Postscript*, trans. David F. Swenson and Walter Lowrie (Princeton, N.J.: Princeton University Press, 1941). The difficulties of verification apply to a subjective or mental referent whether the state of mind is that of the speaker or someone else. Proving the existence of other minds is a standard puzzle in philosophy, and the reliability of introspection is questioned not only by philosophers but by psychologists as well.

3. It is interesting to compare two explanations of Freud's explanation of human behavior via the id, the ego, superego, transference, repression, etc. One such explanation finds the origin of the Freudian apparatus in the discomfort of Jewish intellectuals who were trying to adopt the civility of the high society of Vienna while feeling guilty at their implicit or explicit rejection of their roots in the East European *Stetl*. This interpreter does not hesitate to identify the Freudian id with the term Yid. Another interpreter attributes the character of Freud's theory and activities to the political movements in Vienna at the end of the nineteenth century. For the first, see John Murray Cuddihy's *The Ordeal of Civility* (New York: Basic Books, 1976), and for the second, Carl E. Schorske, *Fin de-Siècle Vienna* (New York: Alfred A. Knopf, 1980).

4. This conjecture receives support from the cross-cultural similarities in synesthesia. See Charles E. Osgood, "The Cross-Cultural Generality of Visual-Verbal Synesthetic Tendencies," *Behavioral Science* 5 (1960): 146–49.

5. Cf. Roger Shattuck, "How to Rescue Literature," *New York Review of Books* 27, no. 6 (17 April 1980): 29–34.

6. In *On Authority and Revelation: The Book on Adler, or A Cycle of Ethico-Religious Essays*, trans. Walter Lowrie (Princeton, N.J.: Princeton University Press, 1955), Kierkegaard raised the question as to how a claim by someone that he had a divine revelation could be verified.

7. See *Max Weber: Essays in Sociology*, ed. and trans. H.H. Gerth and C. Wright Mills (New York: Oxford University Press, 1946).

8. Vilfredo Pareto, arch foe of doctrines that attribute social change to rational action, nevertheless included a "need for logical developments" among the constants of human motivation. Arthur Livingston, ed., *Man and Society* (New York: Dover publications, 1963), § 888.

9. *Fundamental Principles of the Metaphysics of Ethics*, trans. T.K. Abbott, (New York: Longmans, Green, 1926), p. 46.

10. Ibid., p. 56.

11. Richard Rorty, "Pragmatism, Relativism, and Irrationalism," Presidential Address, *Proceedings and Addresses of the American Philosophical Association* 53, no. 6 (August 1980): 719–39, p. 730.

12. Wendel Berry, *The Unsettling of American Culture & Agriculture* (New York: Avon Books, 1977), p. 132.

13. William Graham Sumner, *Folkways* (Boston: Ginn, 1906, 1934, 1940; Dover ed. 1959).

14. *Republic* VII, 518, *The Republic of Plato*, trans. Francis M. Conford, (New York: Oxford University Press, 1945), p. 232.

10

Rational Action and Education

All institutions have suffered losses of credibility in the last decade, and I shall not rehearse the reasons pundits have deduced or dreamed up to account for it. Previous chapters contribute to that litany not from the viewpoint of the pundit but from that of the well-intentioned citizen trying to act rationally in a modern society. The public school has not escaped the credibility loss. It too has been subjected to a drumfire of criticism from various sources, and if the loss of credibility is well founded, the whole democratic dream may be on the verge of a rude awakening. For the school is society's device for inducting each generation into the knowledge and attitudes thought to be necessary for enlightened citizenship. It behooves us, therefore, to probe the factors behind this critism.

In the first place, polls of public opinion still register satisfaction with the public schools, although lack of violent dissatisfaction might be a more accurate estimate. However, the polls aggregate so many different "publics" and so many different schools that the generalizations evaporate into clouds of qualifications. Despite the general charge that the schools have failed, there are many communities in which pupils do learn the basics, and a good deal besides. These schools graduate students who go to college and do well there. These schools are less likely to be found in the inner city than in the suburbs; less likely among the poor than among the. more affluent communities. When aggregated the opinion polls mask differences between school climates and are as misleading as the average temperature of the United States would be of its regional variations. The most reasonable generalization is that the standard curriculum as taught to middle-class children by standard methods have not achieved middle-class results in non-middle-class environments. In this sense, they have not fulfilled the promise implicit in the civil rights legislation of the 1960s.

In the second place, the credibility of a school or school system is as much a function of its clientele as of its program or efficiency. We can compare schools' ability to teach only when pupils are equally prepared to learn. On this basis much of the adverse criticism is misdirected. Perhaps the saddest result of this criticism is disillusionment with the ability of the public school to teach children not ready for standard instruction. We are no longer confident that schooling can repair in one generation centuries of social and economic inequality.

As to causes for the diminished faith in this institution there is no lack of candidates, hypotheses, and villains. One fact should be obvious, namely, that we can no longer identify *the public* which the public school is supposed to serve. There are as many publics as there are constituencies—and there are many constituencies that want the schools to serve *their* particular interests. The civil rights legislation of the mid-1960s has been implemented by school programs designed to meet the needs of minorities, the handicapped, and other disadvantaged groups. These programs, when mandated, fragment the curriculum, and when supported by special federal funds contingent upon compliance, dominate it.[1] As long as the public schools served a public satisfied with a more or less standardized subject-matter curriculum, taught in more or less standardized style, the school had a high degree of credibility. When the consensus of expectation broke down, so did the program, the methodology, and the credibility.

As an institution the school is ancillary to and a surrogate of the family, the community (local and national), and the cultural ethos. When the family, the community, and the culture become diversified, the surrogate function is stalled. Today there is no family model or ideal that the school can represent; there is no uniformity in community mores, and cultural uniformity not only is hard to find but is not even supposed to exist. The surrogate roles of the schools are rarely spelled out, but they give the school a psychological unity of attitude, which in turn it reinforces. When these roles are smudged and the outlines scumbled, the school loses confidence; it does not know what to practice and what to preach.

The loss of clarity in the family, community, and cultural values has resulted in a rush to enroll children in private schools that promise to serve as surrogates for the values of this or that group of parents. Religious schools have always performed this function for a certain portion of the population, but today schools are selected on other grounds as well.

There are schools for children of parents who want them to go to the Ivy League colleges; for those who want formal grammar, spelling, and multiplication tables taught by daily drill; for those who want their children to be creative and not subjected to any drill; for those who believe in creationism as opposed to evolution; and so on. There are private schools for all ideologies and idolatries.

Privatism is preached by libertarians who want parents to have the right to choose schools as they do automobiles or home sites, the best they can afford. And to help every family to a school of its choice, tax credits or tuition credits are recommended. Some argue for a system whereby public moneys are alotted by vouchers to families who can then use them for tuition for schools of their choice.

The surface plausibility of the libertarians' demand for freedom of choice is marred by their forgetfulness. They forget that in this area, as in the economic one, goverment regulation came into being to correct certain evils. They talk as if these evils no longer exist and that government intervention is the only evil. Why freedom of choice would avoid the evils the public school system was created to correct is hard to figure out. The credibility of the libertarians is compromised by their lack of candor. How much of the yearning for freedom to choose a school is fired by the desire to get children away from integrated schools of the inner city?

One would like to think that at least the credibility of the educational establishment as expert in educational science and pedagogy has remained intact. After all, there are colleges of education on the campus of the university. Professors of education do research, write books and articles, and in general behave like other academics. Unfortunately, educational research suffers from a variety of disabilities. First, it shares the theoretical and methodological infirmities of the social sciences that serve as its parent disciplines. As a result, shelves upon shelves of studies document the obvious or outrage common sense; the research comes up with few generalizations that are both new and true. Moreover, the educational enterprise is committed ideologically to meeting individual differences, so that seeking any generalization is, in a sense, wrongheaded to begin with. It may be conjectured that at the subconscious level neither educators nor their clients want to find a genuinely scientific theory of teaching and learning; it would do violence to the unique individuality of persons. Thus the research establishment is in the awkward position of seeking strenuously for what it does not want to find. The net effect of the mountains of research—much of it done by good methodologists—is that today there is neither craft nor theory consensus.[2] That the public still has a great deal of confidence in the schools and in teachers is more a tribute to individual skill and strong instincts of survival of teachers than to educational science.

The credibility of the school as an institution is no greater than the credibility of its personnel. These personnel are divided into administrators, teachers, and sundry clerical and maintenance workers. From the administration the community expects efficient leadership plus enough clarity of mind and strength of character to keep school policy in line with some coherent philosophy of life and education. Just as the school serves surrogate functions for the community, so the administrator is the school's surrogate.

Teachers are supposed to serve pupils directly through instruction. As professionals they are supposed to rationalize their procedures by theories of learning and teaching. As persons they are expected to serve as models of character. If the school loses credibility, the cause must be sought in the unwillingness or inability of administrators and teachers to act out their roles.

As to the administrators, there is a real question whether they have not abdicated their roles as educators in favor of managing the system and maintaining good public relations. Mandates from Washington and state capitols have deprived them of educational authority over the schools. The growth of unions has diminished their authority over teaching personnel. Diverse interest groups among parents have impaired authority over policy. Citizen committees are being asked to meet and recommend the shape of the curriculum and other matters of educational policy. The need for plebiscites on school projects makes it virtually mandatory for the administrator to concentrate on public relations.

One of the most damaging examples of this subservience to political pressures and the lure of federal funds was the acquiescence of school boards and administrators in a strange deal. The terms of the deal were that, given funds for special programs, the public school would equalize educational opportunity for disadvantaged populations. The deal was made even though every one knew that part of the disadvantage of disadvantaged children is their unreadiness to undertake the standard programs in the standard school catering to the children of the middle-class parents. Moreover, everyone knew that to remedy the economic discriminations that caused this unreadiness would require a budget of Pentagonian proportions, and many years of reconstruction. The schools, of course, have failed to deliver on this unbelievable promise, and in the process have forfeited much of their credibility.

The blame for the failure fell on the teachers, teachers who by and large and at best were "trained" to work in standard classrooms, filled with middle-class children, pursuing a more or less standard curriculum. They did not always succeed even when their pupils came to school emotionally and physically ready to undergo instruction—as natural a part of middle-class childhood as seeing the pediatrician and getting shots. To ask teachers to cope with large populations of children who did not fit the standard pattern and to whom the pattern at times seemed threatening was asking for the impossible. As the decade of the late 1960s and early '70s unrolled, "relating" to pupils of different cultures became the key to classroom success. Some have never "related," and some to this day fear physical assaults in their own classrooms. It was as if standard physicians and nurses were asked, almost overnight, to deal with an epidemic about which they knew virtually nothing.

The parallel is misleading because the claim to professional status for the classroom teacher is at best a euphemism for a paraprofessional with a college degree. Even if there were a reliable consensus on the theory of schooling, the average teacher in preservice "training" is reluctant to study what little of it is offered. Theory courses are shouted down as impractical in that "jungle out there." And teaching does not have the benefit of craft consensus such as the plumbers, carpenters, electricians, and auto mechanics enjoy.[3]

With the loss of administrative credibility for leadership in policy, the lack of professional credibility for control of instruction, and the erosion of its surrogatory function, what is left to the public schools as grounds for credibility?

CREDIBILITY OF HIGHER EDUCATION

Before trying to frame a plausible answer to this question, it may be helpful to ask about the credibility of collegiate education. Here the story is somewhat different. The credibility of the scholarly disciplines is high, because academic guilds legitimate themselves by a consensus of the learned in that discipline. The qualifications for a good historian, classicist, chemist, or physicist are clear to the members of the respective disciplines, and they are accepted by the public.

Professional schools enjoy high credibility if their graduates are placed in desirable positions and achieve eminence in their fields. At the moment schools of medicine, law, engineering, commerce, and agriculture enjoy high credibility with the public; schools of education do not.

The college of liberal arts, freestanding or as part of the university, has low credibility for two reasons. One is that liberal studies do not have the vocational payoff that undergraduates expect; the other is that there is some doubt that the faculty really believe in the value of the liberal studies as general education. What credibility they do have accrues from the academic status of the specialists who make up the faculty of the various disciplines.

These developments are not hard to understand. As far as getting a good job is concerned, a general or liberal diploma is far less rewarding than a degree from a professional school. During the late 1960s and early '70s undergraduates played down the vocational factor in schooling. The draft, rather than the desire for a career, kept many young men on the campus. Many of these students came from fairly affluent families, so that earning daily bread was no problem. Furthermore, the ideological steaminess of the period deflated economic values in favor of the more humanistic ones, so that getting a job was not high on the list of adolescent priorities. Finally, the revolt against all establishments included disdain for the Protestant work ethic. It was more human or humanistic to drift across the country on a motorcycle or to hitchhike more or less where the spirit moved, to run away from home, than to be tied to a steady job.

The liberal studies prospered during the period. The social sciences, philosophy, literature, black studies, women's studies, environmental studies, enjoyed a boom. Literature classes were theaters of social protest. Young faculty members in these fields were among the leaders of campus protest movements. Large numbers of Ph.D. candidates filled advanced seminars in the hope of becoming college professors themselves. Expanding undergraduate enrollments made these expectations seem far more realistic than they turned out to be.

The late 1970s saw a reversal of most of these attitudes toward higher education. Students, young women as well as the males, became interested in economic values. Their expectations for standards of living rose sharply from indifference to luxury to a passion for them. They adopted the values of the "beautiful people" produced for the middle-class trade by the fashion industry and glorified by mass media advertising.

For a long time after the colonial period, the four-year liberal arts college, although it served as a preprofessional school for the ministry, law, and other callings, was primarily a maturing vat in which young adolescents of good family ripened into older adolescents. The goal of their studies was neither vocation nor scholarship but an education suitable to cultivation of the mind—liberal in the Aristotelian sense of being free from the constraints of vocational and other obligations. The classic works in the various intellectual disciplines were studied for their contribution to wisdom, virtue, and taste—attributes desirable for membership in a social class destined for leadership in government and industry. Exposure to the best that had been thought and written would suffuse the mind with kindred qualities. The liberal studies were supposed to produce the man of enlightened virtue with capacity not only for citizenship but leadership as well. And if one reads the catalogues of liberal arts colleges and the colleges of the liberal arts in the university, the same language making the same claims will still be found there.

These claims have lost much of their credibility in recent years, not wholly because students have returned to a desire for the material values of life. Repeatedly surveys of college graduates indicate a belief in the value of the liberal studies and a wish that they had taken more of them during their undergraduate years. They seem to regret that the pressure of professional specialization restricted these studies.

There is a general impression abroad that the liberal studies can be picked up later, without tuition. After all, most of them are couched in ordinary language. In the conflict between the two cultures it was often pointed out that scientists can read literature but poets cannot read science or mathematics. Liberal studies by their very claim to be general fostered the notion that no special ability or instruction was needed to appropriate them. If this argument is valid, then the liberal studies prescribed as part of general education have a dubious claim on the time of the undergraduate. They can be postponed until after professional life has been established, and if that takes up all of one's time, then they can be postponed until retirement. Indeed, the ideal customer for a liberal education is the well-to-do retiree, not the young.

The faith in the vague promises of liberal education lingers even though the historical evidence as to its benefits is ambiguous. Many who have undergone the traditional program of such studies have not been distinguished for their wisdom, taste, or character. On the contrary, some of history's greatest villains have had the benefits of a liberal education.

By the usual criteria, liberal studies taken in college do not seem effective. The amount retained after a few years is small. And the ability to apply the principles of the various disciplines to life situations is not impressive. Few who have had the standard courses in the sciences and arts can use them to solve problems. Understanding the principles of the internal combustion engine is of little use if one cannot locate the carburetor or lacks the appropriate tools. The knowledge nonspecialists use to solve problems with automobiles is that of the telephone directory—the yellow pages, of course. The liberal studies need a rationale that explains how they function in life.[4]

The undergraduate's attitude toward the liberal studies is reinforced by the faculty teaching those studies. They are recruited from the pool of Ph.D.s in a discipline—history, literature, the social sciences, philosophy—who want to become respected figures in their particular version of the discipline—specialists. The classicist whose professional career is the study of a given Latin text is as much a professional and specialist as the electrical engineer and the veterinarian. He is no more humanistic than they are, and with prestige and salary geared to specialism and recognition by the guild, they are as much intellectual entrepreneurs as any members of the professional faculties.

While once it was the broadly and liberally trained educator who seemed to inhabit an ivory tower, today it is the superspecialist in fields ranging from economics to psychology to physics who is most out of touch with reality. While contemporary work-place problems are ignorant of departmental structures of universities, today's overspecialized scholar is blissfully unaware of what his colleagues are up to—even in closely related fields. Indeed, young scholars revel in their provincial ignorance, holding it up as a sign of their "scientific" professionalism. When asked how their work relates to another discipline or to a practical problem, they joyously declare, "Who cares?"[5]

Teaching undergraduates in general studies courses is not a mark of accomplishment to such specialists; only the gifted major who might become a Ph.D. candidate is really worth the investment of their time and interest. Undergraduates know all this; they pick it up from the formal gossip emanating from the faculty Senate and from the informal gossip of graduate teaching assistants.

In the light of all these considerations, it is not at all unthinkable that in time only preprofessional studies in any of the liberal arts disciplines will be offered in the university. Liberal arts colleges are already inventing and frantically advertising the preprofessional values of such courses, and community college faculty will probably be more suitable and willing to provide undergraduate instruction in "general studies" than college professors. Of course there is really no reason why general education cannot be completed in the high school, especially if a thirteenth grade is provided for the purpose, and the school devotes itself to it.

In the light of what has been argued in previous chapters with regard to the credibility problems of the specialized scholars and professionals as far as the enlightened citizen is concerned, it becomes evident that educationally the crucial loci of credibility are the liberal studies. If the remoralization of and by education is to come about, it will have to be through studies that are relevant to wisdom, taste, and character; to existential as well as to propositional truth.

One way of rethinking this problem is to give more attention to the ways in which knowledge, and especially the kind of knowledge acquired in school, is used. Some of what we study we retain as learned and recall on appropriate occasions. Some learnings, such as theories, we apply to solve problems. Both uses are central to vocational education. We learn facts, theories, and skills that we use in our occupations pretty much as they were studied in the classroom. At the professional level we not only learn theory but also skill in the technology by which the theory is applied to practice. These replicative and applicative uses of learning are explicit: output can be matched with input. They are species of *knowing that*, *knowing how*, and *knowing why*.

But there are other uses of schooling, especially of general education. Elsewhere I have called them the associative and interpretive uses. Associatively, one stocks concepts and images to build the many layers of meaning by which life is felt, understood, and evaluated. All experience contributes to this imagic-conceptual store, but the arts are preeminently suited to this purpose. Learning how to use the resources of the arts is the business of aesthetic education. The marks and signs of credibility are shaped out of images of character. In a world such as our children are likely to inhabit, the arts are more than a luxury or refinement; they are necessary to make the truth existentially significant.

Along with the associative uses of schooling go the interpretive ones. The study of the intellectual disciplines as part of general education is not for application to vocation or other problems of life. Only specialized knowledge and mastery of special technologies can *solve* problems or relieve the predicaments out of which the standard problems of life emerge. The contexts in which life has to be lived, in which problems have to be construed, and in which truth has to be evaluated and commitment made are supplied by the conceptual systems and modes of inquiry of the disciplines. The disciplines studied explicitly in school become resources used tacitly in life; their details are forgotten, leaving frames or lenses or stencils of interpretation, both of fact and value. Perspective and context are the functional residues of general education. We understand *with* them, even though we are not attending to them. I believe that a convincing case can be made for the functionality of formal course work in the associative and interpretive uses of knowledge, even though the content of the formal courses cannot be recalled on cue.[6]

Until these differences in the uses of schooling are clarified and appreciated, undergraduates and the general public will respect them more for reputation than usefulness. The academic specialists will continue to regard a liberal education as a poor substitute for scholarship, and the university administration will alternate between neglect of the liberal studies and guilt. In witness whereof, every twenty-five years or so Harvard institutes a reexamination of general education, which other institutions feel obliged to imitate. Within five years the eminent faculty recruited for the program are back in their labs and library carrels.

The loss of credibility by the public schools and by the liberal arts curriculum in higher education differ in an important way. In the latter it is not due to the lack of expertise on the part of the academicians, but rather to their specialism; the loss of credibility in the public school is blamed on incompetence, usually the alleged incompetence of the classroom teacher. Although it is always safe to admit that some classroom teachers are incompetent, the question is what under the current circumstances are the criteria of competence.

Under the present circumstances, for reasons that have been mentioned, there are no surrogatory functions that the school can assume with any confidence. There seems to be no area of instruction or discipline in which the school authorities can claim autonomy. The autonomy that colleges and universities enjoy with respect to their disciplines the schools do not have and do not dare to claim.

"The curriculum of American schools is shaped by many forces beyond the systematic efforts of curriculum developers to create new courses. Laws, court decisions, wars, social trends, economic conditions, political conflicts, changes in the public mood, and other influences beyong the school setting can and do affect what is taught."[7] This comment taken from a volume reporting a National Institute of Education Task Force on curriculum issues, is an accurate description of the loss of autonomy of the public school. With it has gone the possibility of evaluating the competence of teachers, because to judge a math or reading teacher presuposses some consensus on the structure and contents of these subjects and the methods of teaching them. If a math teacher is judged by the ability to control the classroom or involve parents in school activities or help pupils get off drugs, then the structure and content and purpose of math study become irrelevant; if the teacher cannot maintain discipline, content and purpose become irrelevant. The breakdown of the authority of the school over the content of the curriculum and methods of instruction makes a shambles of all efforts to evaluate schools or teachers, a shambles that elaborate testing programs cannot repair.

There is a way out of the chaos, but it requires recognition that certain aspects of schooling are free *by right* from the approval of the citizens. If there are areas of instruction that have a legitimation of their own, then there may be areas of autonomy without the onus of arbitrary indoctrination and imposition. Assertions warranted by the methods of science would certainly have a strong claim to such autonomy, but there may also be areas of legitimate autonomy in disciplines that deal with the human reality, with existential as well as propositional truth.

The disciplines from which the content of liberal studies is taken also have their legitimation in the consensus of the learned. The content of philosophy, history, and literature have undergone continuous critical sifting. Although the value of these contents may vary in the estimate of scholars from time to time, the judgments are informed, expert judgments, not arbitrary preferences. These disciplines, as well as the scientific ones, are not validatable by a consensus of parents or citizens. Although there is no predicting or interdicting what a school committee will do, it is difficult to imagine that it will determine the nature of good mathematics or chemistry or physics by a majority vote. They may, however, see no impropriety in voting on what constitutes good biology, especially as regards the origin of species, and in the humanities and social sciences they are likely to feel free to vote on the propriety of any topic, book or author. The closer a discipline comes to existential truth, the more the citizen feels entitled to challenge the experts, especially if they challenge deep-seated moral convictions. The citizen is ambivalent with respect to relativism in moral matters. He welcomes the modish methodological relativism of the social sciences insofar as it gives him liberty to hold on to his own views of right and wrong, good and evil. But what *he* considers to be right and wrong does not seem to be relative or subjective at all, and those who disagree are simply misguided or corrupt. When it comes to the study of the humanities the public claims the right to challenge the school authorities on the works being studied and how they are taught.

This misapprehension the school must correct, or it may as well give up the pretense of doing general or liberal education. It is the responsibility of the school—administration, school board, teachers—to make clear to the public the difference between the intellectual quality of a discipline and its usefulness to society. The latter is a political issue, the former is a scholarly one. The political issue is subject to the will of the people; the scholarly issue is not, and if in this area, including the humanities, the school does not have a measure of autonomy, it cannot assume responsibility for general education.

Given this autonomy in the disciplines and to some extent in the methods of teaching them, judgments on teacher competence and the quality of schooling become manageable and intelligible. If, on the contrary, the curriculum disintegrates into activities, projects, innovative exercises of one kind or another, so do the criteria for evaluating them. As usual, while the process is being debated, the product sinks to secondary importance.

The claim to autonomy for the teacher carries a price. First, teachers have to be sufficiently qualified in the scholarship of a discipline to make judgments of quality in that discipline. Second, there has to be a strong— almost unquestioned—commitment to defend the right of the school and its personnel to this autonomy. At the collegiate level these conditions are pretty well fulfilled; much less so in the public school.

EDUCATION FOR CITIZENSHIP

General education, from kindergarten through grade 12, based on the study of the disciplines, the public schools could manage if the community permitted concentration on it, and if the school population arrived at the schoolhouse ready and more or less willing to receive it. Individual differences in learning rate could be met by ability grouping based on achievement (rather than IQ) and not by varying the content of the curriculum, as is the current practice. Much of the ineptness of the public school results from the effort to provide an unlimited variety of instruction to meet an indefinite list of real or imagined pupil needs.

Nevertheless, the education of the citizen who is to participate in a democratic society requires more than the interpretive and associative resources furnished by general education. It requires the skills of collective deliberation and decision, which utilize the content of general studies. What can the school do about skills of this kind?

Dewey's Complete Act of Thought furnishes a design for acquiring and practicing such skills. The school can teach groups how to convert their predicaments into problems, to observe and sharpen the conditions relevant to the problem, suggest hypotheses, predict their consequences, and set up "experimental" actions to verify or disconfirm them.

Learning how to think scientifically and critically has always been regarded as the proper goal of schooling by those who have little use for rote learning. Some would make practice of the CAT on "real" projects *the* curriculum; but just as rote learning cannot be relied upon to produce good thinking automatically as a by-product, so cannot good thinking be relied upon to produce the knowledge needed to think with.

Although the style and structure of the CAT is the same for all problems, the knowledge needed to apply the CAT to large social problems is not the same as will do in more limited ones. On which side of the street to construct a new sewer line can be debated and decided with the knowledge and judgment available to the homeowners directly concerned. The necessary engineering knowledge and skill are also available locally. But how to dispose of atomic wastes or the wastes of toxic industrial products is not a problem to which local resources, physical, financial, or intellectual, are adequate.

The CAT when applied to any but relatively simple problems requires knowledge that, as a rule, comes from formal study. This knowledge explicitly or tacitly provides the generalizations needed to generate hypotheses. If, for example, a situation requires a knowledge of chemistry, physics, or biology in order to frame plausible hypotheses, someone in the group had better have taken some physics, chemistry, or biology. Common-sense knowledge will not go very far toward fashioning hypotheses in the complex social problems that confront a modern society.

When, however, there is or has been systematic study of the disciplines, the CAT becomes a way of testing its effectiveness. A complete curriculum, therefore, would include not only the mastery of symbolic skills of information and the basic concepts of selected subject matters but also a problem-solving strand that uses the CAT as a method of group deliberation on selected social problems.[8]

Given adequate autonomy over the curriculum, the school could make good the promise that high school graduates would be able to think individually and collectively about current social problems in a rational and informed way. The disciplines would provide perspectival knowledge to think with, the CAT would provide the form of problem solving. Whether the CAT can cope with the obstacles to rational action in our society is another matter.

One more strand is needed for citizenship education, and this does not come automatically from the disciplines or the CAT. Fruitful collective deliberation presupposes some agreement on the common good. The criteria of a good society have to function tacitly or explicitly in order for the CAT to become a form of social action. For Dewey the criteria of a good community were "How numerous and varied are the interests which are consciously shared?"[9] Current demands for participatory democracy, however, do not stress a common good or shared interests; the emphasis is on the diversity and autonomy of interests. When different constituencies in the city disagree on the control of the schools, the solution has been to split up districts so that each group has its own educational turf. And if majority decisions do not please groups or subgroups, protests, disruptions, and civil disobedience are regarded as acceptable responses.

Participatory democracy becomes a contest of wills, not a sharing of them. With the proliferation of singly-interest groups, each using its votes whenever and wherever they promote that interest, orthodox democracy and political liberalism are having a bad time. The battle royal of the political arena is not a good model for citizenship education. For that, the school needs a community of shared interests.

The prospect for such unity is not bright. The trend toward pluralism is stronger; the new ethnicity, the new individualism, and the new fragmentation promise little unity or even a common theme on which many variations could be played.

Some of the reasons for this have already been discussed. Chief among them is the sheer inability of even well-intentioned intellectuals, statesmen, and economic leaders to anticipate all the consequences that any widespread change would entrain. It is virtually impossible to isolate the effects of such changes. Another is that limited resources cannot provide all competing groups with equal benefits or prevent unequal sacrifices. Still another, and not an insignificant one, is the readiness of unscrupulous groups and individuals to take advantage of any cooperative arrangement that might be reached. Finally, there are genuine ideological differences, and it is to the political as well as ideological advantage of these groups not to find unifying solutions.

One is tempted to take refuge in the ancient doctrine that there is a universal human nature, an Aristotelian form, a *telos*, that every individual in the species is striving to actualize. This form is the formula for human happiness, for the organization of appetite, emotion, and reason into a life of virtue. The humanities are the disciplines usually identified with this enterprise. Unfortunately, the idea of *a* human nature is itself one of our most controversial topics. There is as yet no decisive way of distinguishing the effects of nature and nurture.

And yet the notion need not be abandoned. Whether by genes or learning, human beings have evolved remarkably constant value systems. It is not unreasonable to speculate that if certain values have remained constant for a long time, then it may be that through natural selection, those who did not develop them have been eliminated. Certain sexual mores, for example, may have survived because extreme variations from them have interfered with the reproductive processes sufficiently to be eliminated from the gene pool. The fact of survival does not ensure moral worth; some traits may have survived that might as well have been eliminated from "human nature."

There is perhaps a better reason for not giving up on the idea of a human essence, a generic form of humanity, which individual lives more or less approximate. It is the fact that for centuries the search for this essence has gone on. If this search is an illusion, it is certainly one of our most persistent ones. Another possible factor in the durability of the notion is the tendency toward conceptual constancy. For example, is a culture values courage, it will define "human" and "goodness" so that individuals who do not understand or appreciate the general characteristics of courage will be classified as inhuman or nonhuman. The group will reward behavior that has these general properties and punish behavior that does not. And so natural selection of a sort goes on. Those character traits that serve as survival markers can be called the virtues, excellences of character that define the good personality and indirectly, the good society.

So construed we can understand why there is a remarkable constancy in the basic virtues, and a no less remarkable variety in the definitions of the behaviors that are allowed to count as instances of these virtues. Courage is always an admirable trait, a virtue, but the behaviour that will qualify as courageous differs from time to time and probably from culture to culture. It can take the form of physical steadiness in the face of danger, but in a sophisticated culture it may be interpreted as the willingness not to face a physical danger if it endangers a friend or an ideal. Each epoch takes a hand in the redefinition. The arts help the imagination invent and contemplate new forms of bravery, honesty, temperance, wisdom, and so forth, as well as the corresponding vices. Value education, as differentiated from value training or conditioning, is concerned primarily with arguments as to whether particular behaviors do or do not fill the definitional requirements of a given virtue. The social order relies on the introjection by the individual of the group's current behavioral qualifications for a given virtue. Ethics, religion, and moral reflection in general test the consistency of these qualifications.

The humanities, including literature, history, and philosophy, represent the learned tradition in the systematic examination, critique, and redefinition of the virtues and the diverse formulae for the good life. This tradition, although not free from silly solemnity, pedantry, and pretense, still has high credibility in the realm of truth about value—existential truth. Regardless of time and circumstance, the schools at all levels can induct the young into this consensus with the confidence that it is about as near as we can get to an abiding, if not absolute, truth about the good life.

This, of course, is traditional classical humanism, and it combines both propositional and existential rationality. Some version of this outlook is about the only sort of unity on which the school can build its curriculum and justification. One version that brings it closer to the American tradition of enlightenment and democracy can be found in what Gunnar Myrdal in *An American Dilemma*[10] called the American Creed, and it may be profitable to probe the possibilities of that notion to restore to the schools its role in education for citizenship.

REFERENCES

1. *See* J.M. Atkin, "The Government in the Classroom," *Daedalus* 109 (Summer 1980): 85–98; and Jon Schaffarzick and Gary Sykes, eds., *Value Conflicts and Curriculum Issues* (Berkeley, Calif.: McCutchan, 1979).

2. H.S. Broudy, "The Fiduciary Basis of Education: A Crisis in Credibility," *Phi Delta Kappan* 59, no. 2 (October 1977): 87–90.

3. I have belabored these melancholy theses in many articles and a few books. For more detailed arguments, *see The Real World of the Public Schools*, (New York: Harcourt, Brace, Jovanovich, 1972), and "What Do Professors of Education Profess?" the DeGarmo Lecture, *Educational Forum* 44, no. 4 (May 1980): 441–51.

4. A brief outline of such a rationale will be attempted later in the chapter. A more detailed analysis can be found in my "Tacit Knowing as a Rationale for Liberal Education," *Teachers College Record* 80, no. 3 (1979): 446–62.

5. James O'Toole, "Education Is Education, and Work Is Work—Shall Ever the Twain Meet?" *Teachers College Record* 81, no. 1 (Fall 1979): 20.

6. *See* "Tacit Knowing as a Rationale for Liberal Education."

7. Jon Schaffarzick, *Op. cit.*, p. 25.

8. The details of such a curriculum have been set forth in H.S. Broudy, B.O. Smith, and J.R. Burnett, *Democracy and Excellence in American Secondary Education*, (Chicago: Raund McNally, 1964). Reprint Edition (Huntington, N.Y., J.R. Krieger, 1978).

9. *Democracy and Education* (New York: Macmillan, 1916) p. 96.

10. New York: Harper & Bros., 1944.

11

Education, Truth, and Credibility

If credibility is to be a factor in the citizen's ability to act rationally, then the school's emphasis on truth, that is, warranted assertion, has to be balanced by teaching for warranted commitment. What would such teaching be like? Where is the content of such study to be found? How will it fit into a curriculum sensitive to the constraints of a pluralistic society?

The grounds for credibility are purity of heart, freedom from envy and hypocrisy, sincerity, authenticity. These character traits are not observable to the outsider; even the self, of which they are characteristics, cannot always be sure what they are and what they mean. The outsider can only guess at the motives of an action, calculate the consequences, and in these indirect ways check the sincerity of the actor. Investigating committees arrive at such inferences by examining witnesses, documents, and the like.

This kind of inquiry is a species of critical thinking and can be carried on by anyone who has a sense of consistency and familiarity with the substance of the issues under consideration. For example, to ascertain the purity of heart of those involved in a huge financial swindle requires an understanding of the ways of the financial world. However, it is this kind of detailed technical knowledge that the citizen cannot acquire easily, even if the information is plentiful and available. To anyone not familiar with the financial world, the *Wall Street Journal* reports might as well have been written in a foreign language. Even if he can construe the syntax of statements such as Company X has been charged with fraud by the SEC in its efforts to acquire a controlling interest in Company Y by offering tempting stock options to Mr. Z, a former director of Company Q, their import remains opaque.

The citizen relies on the credibility of the *Journal* and accepts its conclusions without really understanding the evidence for it. Nevertheless, the citizen, if he is really literate and if his general education has given his some understanding of economic concepts, should be able to make some sense out of these reports and some estimate of their truthfulness. But if the experts disagree, his task is to decide which, if any, he can trust. As has been noted, such judgments depend on conjectures as to motives and interests.

A similar situation confronts the citizen in political decisions, but there is a difference between Voter X deciding which of two candidates he can believe and which of two parties he can support. In the former case, the credibility inference could be grounded on knowing what each candidate has done in the past. Knowing their value hierarchies and their tendencies toward consistency, honesty, and trruthfulness, the citizen makes his choice on which to believe and trust. In the latter situation, the voter must examine not only the record but also whether the professed ideology of the parties is sincerely held and whether it conforms to a value hierarchy to which the voter is committed.

The difference in the requirements of these two judgments is reflected in the role of formal schooling for credibility. The school cannot provide the positive knowledge of particular situations, parties, and persons needed to predict what a candidate would do, but it can explore the principles governing the motives of the virtuous man and the good citizen. Where in the curriculum can one look for such content?

THE CREDIBILITY CURRICULUM

If the sciences, physical and social, are the sources of warranted assertion as to matters of *physical* fact, the humanities claim to be the sources of warranted belief about *value* fact. Literature, history, the arts, philosophy, and religion have sifted critically the attempts to get at the essence and peculiarities of human nature, its excellences and deficiencies, and the targets of its commitment. Some of these materials aim at generalization about the nature of the good life (e.g., as in moral philosophy). Some, like history and literature, present personages and events so as to reveal character types. There was a time during the Renaissance when young men were inspired to imitate the deeds of the heroes of history and myth. "Throughout the length and breadth of Italy, memorials of ancient greatness spurred her children on to emulation. Ghosts of Roman patriots and poets seemed hovering around their graves, and calling on posterity to give them life again . . . generating an acute desire for fame . . . ." [1]

I am, of course, using the term "humanities" as employed by departments of humanities in institutions of higher education. The meaning has changed over the centuries as various interpretations of humanism had their vogue. Cicero meant by the word the study of Greek and Roman letters or literature. These works were humanizing factors in that they already embodied, or were thought to embody, the essense of human culture. Hence for Cicero, *humanitas* meant education of man as such. Presumably, those who were ignorant of Greek and Roman letters were still in the state of *barbaritas*, outsiders.[2]

Formal schooling has tried to incorporate the humanities into its curriculum. Stories, fables, and proverbs were the vehicles in the earlier years; in later years selections from the classic literatures were studied; in higher education, courses, curricula and even departments carried the humanities label. As has been indicated at several points in this volume, the notion of liberal education or liberal studies persists in our own country, although the "better" the university in academic terms, the less enthusiasm one finds among the specialists in humanistic studies to teach them in the liberal spirit to undergraduates. Nevertheless, the typical undergraduate program does include courses in the subjects commonly classed with the humanities. What I have called existential truth, the kind most relevant to the credibility question, is encountered in literature, history, the arts, and in philosophy, especially in courses in ethics and moral philosophy.[3]

The public schools in recent years were enlisted in a revival of moral education in which Values Clarification techniques and Lawrence Kohlberg's version of Piaget's stages of cognitive development figured prominently.[4] The success of these efforts remains to be demonstrated. So far the crime rate, use and abuse of drugs, the incidence of venereal disease, and adolescent pregnancy show little reduction. Although the future may warrant a more optimistic assessment, it seems to be a melancholy fact that in corrupt communities, moral education programs in the schools have little redemptive effect. In communities that are not corrupt, the programs formalize and reinforce habits and attitudes already formed outside the school.

One should not become cynical about the value of formal study of ethics or the logic of moral discourse prematurely. It may be that this kind of study functions tacitly rather than explicitly. The theories and arguments studied in courses on moral or ethical theory may not be recollectable later in life, but those who have had such formal study interpret life situations differently from those who have not. And it may just be that all of general or liberal education functions in this way. It suggests a type of cognition that bridges the gap between propositional and existential truth.

TACIT KNOWING AND CREDIBILITY

Michael Polanyi's theory of tacit knowing[5] holds that in all knowing there is a *focal* awareness of meaning to which many elements contribute *subsidiarily* and *tacitly*. Thus numerous sensory and conceptual clues contribute tacitly to the explicit perception of an object and an understanding of it. The tacit component need not be consciously attended to. We think and feel *with* the tacit element, even though we do not necessarily feel or know it explicitly. Educationally, the significant point is that some learnings can function tacitly.

It is in this sense that Polanyi argues that all knowledge is personal. A tacit factor, which may be cognitive or affective, guides our hypotheses and judgment, even in the most highly organized and objective scientific endeavor. A sense of coherence, relevance, reality, and importance is such a tacit component and determines why a scientist pursues one line of inquiry rather than another. Just such a sense could be the tacit clue to the credibility of a proposition or theory. Thus, if I employ tacit clues that characterize Jones as not capable of embezzling the funds of the church, arguments and proofs of the contrary will seem incredible. We might say that our moral intuitions are tacit schemata for credibility in general (i.e., for warranted belief). Knowledge about probable motivation or human nature, accordingly, would have a profound effect in judging the truthfulness of assertions made by parties to a controversy or by the actions of legislators, business groups, and other agencies. Such knowledge, studied formally in school, may or may not be made explicit.

The tacit knowing hypothesis may throw some light on the intuitive resisitance to distinctions and separations that specialists like to draw, for example, between moral and legal issues or between moral and economic questions. Although we can conceive the separation *in mente*, we suspect the motives of those who insist on it. One possible explanation of this attitude is that the mores of the group or the ethos of a nation may operate tacitly on all judgments and actions. They may favor judgments that on purely logical or practical grounds might be rejected, and vice versa. Thus the importance of national honor may override pragmatic considerations. Machiavellians command our admiration for clarity of thought and refusal to allow moral considerations to affect them, but it is a grudging admiration at best.

The interplay of tacit and explicit factors may be the key to the role of schooling in credibility. One characteristic of this interplay is that an item of knowledge cannot function tacitly and explicitly simultaneously. As Polanyi noted, we can attend to the two slightly different pictures in a stereoptican, in which event the single blended image will disappear. Or we can attend to the latter and the former will disappear.

Analogously, we can teach the humanities, or any subject, for that matter, explicitly and later in life have them function tacitly while our explicit attention is on a problem. In credibility judgments there are also explicit and tacit components. As a rule, formal schooling concentrates on explicit instruction. The effectiveness of such instruction depends on whether an attitude is formed that makes a difference in judgment and action. But formal schooling is also supposed to provide cognitive instruments for appraising and criticizing attitudes.

This interplay between the cognitive and attitudinal factors in credibility is largely an interplay between facts and a value schemata or hierarchy. In the value component external influences play an important, if not decisive, role. The mores of the community, the tastes and preferences conditioned by the home, and the more generalized ethos of the society contribute to the value schema of the individual. They determine to a decisive extent the effect of formal instruction in these areas.

The interplay between the tacit and explicit phases of experience is reflected in the differences between moral education and moral training. The former is explicit, cognitive, logical; the latter is tacit, habitual, highly affective. Each can move into focus; and when it does, the other moves out to the periphery and becomes tacit. When we are analyzing moral discourse and action, the tacit "feeling" of what is right and wrong controls the conclusions as well as the logic. When we are caught in an impulse to act out of righteous indignation tacitly, the logic of the situation may limit the impulse and the action. Although most of the clamor for moral education tends to emanate from parents who really want moral training (i.e., habituation in the mores of the community), effective moral education requires both affective and reflective components in an explicit-tacit interplay.

One expects this combination to take place in the school. Private boarding schools bring it off rather well. Public schools do not, but they can approximate something like it if the home and community form and reinforce the mores. This allows the school to give formal instruction in the principles of morality and to examine them critically for consistency and adequacy, typical topics in ethics. The school can also examine the application of these principles in individual and social life. This kind of reflection compares the behavior tolerated in the community with its professed codes of morality. But what if the school cannot take for granted either the habit formation of the home and community, on the one hand, or its professed ideals, on the other? Much of the difficulty of the public school today can be traced to its inability to give affirmative answers to either or both of these questions. In short, without a strong attitudinal tacit component formed by the home and reinforced by the community, explicit instruction in ethics and values may be no more than preachment.

The mores function tacitly to counter the de-moralization of self-serving specialism. A national ethos counters social fragmentation. It tacitly interposes the common good as a yardstick of context. Formal schooling can teach the content of this ethos explicitly and the intellectual means for reflecting critically upon it. What ethos can the American public school assume? On what value set are Americans so united that it can qualify as the American way?

A reliable formula for national unification is a war, usually presented as a defensive war for survival. With notable exceptions, it rallies the people for sacrifice of life and material gratification as nothing else seems able to do. Perhaps it is war's ability to equalize sacrifice that makes the appeal credible; perhaps the thought of being conquered is so replusive, so threatening, that even some inequalities of sacrifice are accepted so as not to impair the war effort. A common enemy unites a people in a way that a common goal does not. The danger the enemy poses is unambiguous; a common good has to be interpreted and divided, and that causes dissension. However, just wars of self-defense are hard to come by these days.

What about the democratic ideal? At the moment, it is difficult to formulate a definition of democracy that would not be as divisive as the diversity it is intended to unify. The term is invoked by Marxists and Republicans as well as by various gangs of terrorists and revolutionaries. Democracy is used to justify freedom for libertarians who say they want no interference by government and liberals who see the salvation of democracy in greater concern of the government for social justice. Democracy pervades the ideological and dialectical cannotation of freedom.

It is doubtful, for example, that Dewey's concept of democracy as a way of life, of schooling, of a community organization in which a maximum number and variety of interests become sharable, would find general acceptance today. To many individuals, sharing does not mean equal sharing. There is no common pool of goods and services that waits to be apportioned, but rather a pool already apportioned. Any change that disturbs that apportionment will be resisted by those who stand to lose. Nor is there any assurance that a reapportionment would result in a fairer distribution, for reasons that have been repeated so often in the previous chapters. Nor is it clear that any effective principle of unification can be less than international in scope.

THE RETREAT TO SELF

The difficulty of formulating a social or political ideal that would keep diverse value domains relevant to one another inevitably throws the individual back on himself as the organizing principle of life.

Several conceptions of self have already been discussed, and not all of them are equally promising as principles of unification. Between selves two relationships obtain or can obtain that make a society of selves possible. One is empathy by which one self can imagine the state of another and thus engender sympathy. The second is respect for selfhood as an existential condition. The first is limited to a small circle of individuals, and as the circle becomes extended, the intensity of sympathy through empathy becomes more and more diluted. The second is, in a way of speaking, universal for it does not depend on what a particular person has done or will do, but rather on a capacity of the species. This capacity for universalizability was discussed in connection with the Kantian categorical imperative, namely, the respect that persons command by virtue of being able to subject themselves to a moral law of their own making.

The very existence of a sense of moral obligation implies the possibility of assessing inclinations by a moral principle. To have such a sense of obligation, argued Kant, presupposes that human selves can subject themselves freely to a law that is binding on themselves and on all others. Hence the categorical imperative to act only on the maxim that one's principle of action could become a universal law. But such a "legislator" belongs to a kingdom of ends who are never to be treated as a means merely.

If credibility (warranted commitment) is to be rooted in the nature of the self, how the self is defined makes a difference. On the one hand, the self can be self-enclosed, closed off from the intrusion of others. A primal privacy keeps some aspects of experience free from the oversight of others, the law, and other social institutions. Its uniqueness precludes reducing any human individual to an undifferentiated unit. Its way of living in the world is irreplaceable. On the other hand, existence does not establish the right to exist. It has to be acknowledged by those who could in fact deny it. This right, therefore, has to be grounded in selfhood as a universal principle, and this principle is supplied by the respect it generates as a potential legislator of a universal moral law.

These distinctions are necessary because many of the current claims to privacy, liberation, and individual rights are based on psychological grounds. One wants to be free from this or that restraint, but of itself this does not establish the right to be freed from it. The respect for persons morally is grounded in their ability to control their inclinations and not in rejecting such control.

The search for a criterion that would guide the citizen in both warranted assertion and warranted commitment can be stated as attempts to unify fact and value, self and society, the one and the many. They are not reducible to each other or to a third solvent in life or logic. So far as the school, the American public school, is concerned, there is no social, economic, or philosophical theory that it can use as a guide for curriculum or methods of instruction. Yet in the structure of the self there are tendencies that the school might exploit.

Selves are the sources of possibility and therefore of possible actuality. They are a source of being, but they also limit that being by a strain toward consistency, which is at the core of all rationality. The imagination that exfoliates the wildest fantasies is akin in kind to the self that dismisses them as fantasies, because it has also invented science and logic in order to satisfy the impulse to consistency and coherence. The consistency is not only logical; there is an equally strong strain toward moral consistency, a desire to have thought, feeling, and action comport well with ideals and norms of character. The ideal of democracy in our times, if it is to be a unifying principle, must find that principle within the nature of the human self, and its inherent strain toward consistency may be out best strategy for enlightened commitment and warranted assertion.

THE AMERICAN CREED

A suggestion for such a strategy is found in an observation by the Swedish economist, Gunnar Myrdal, in a study of racial problems in the United States.[6] He was impressed by the strange amalgam of ideas and attitudes that he found in the writings of the Founding Fathers and subsequent defenders of the American experiment on the new continent. He called this amalgam the American Creed. It includes sentiments about the essential dignity of man, of his perfectibility, confidence in the consent of the governed, decision by the majority, respect for governance of all phases of life by law coupled with a careless observance of these laws. He traced these ingredients to the English common law, certain principles of Christianity, and political philosophies of the Enlightenment. These have found expression in the Declaration of Independence and in our Constitution. Myrdal regards the American Creed as the most explicit set of ideals a modern society has ever had.

He noted also that all political parties had recourse to the Creed for justification of their policies. Rich and poor, liberals and conservatives, invoked it, although by and large he thought it to be more progressive and liberal in spirit than conservative. The heroes of American history have been reformers in the name of the American Creed, although conservatives can find much in it for their own philosophy of government.

This Creed, according to Myrdal, is the source of what he called high-level valuations or norms of the society. They are stated in general terms (liberty, equality, and what the French later called fraternity), and to these values the people have unswerving loyalty. They are emotionally conditioned and not arguable. On another level, however, beliefs about specific policies of legislation are arguable, and much of the argument revolves around their consistency with the higher-level valuations. Thus debate on a taxation bill sooner or later would come down to arguing whether it was consistent with the American way, freedom, justice, equality, and so on. Both sides would want to claim that their side was more so than the opposition. Neither side, however much the fate of the legislation affected the interests of their group, wants to be branded as being inconsistent with the American Creed.

There is another source of inconsistency, namely, between what Myrdal called beliefs about the social reality and the norms of the Creed. Myrdal found that many of the beliefs about blacks did not accord with the facts, and that some of the facts did not accord with the principles of the Creed.

Myrdal's faith in a democratic society's ability to effect social change rested on this strain toward consistency between legislation and the higher-order evaluations. Lack of such consistency, when made apparent and public, he held, would create a pressure for reform in the direction of the higher, more general values. Education should promote this desire for consistency and the ability of the citizenry to detect inconsistency. But it also argues for an unequivocal commitment to the American Creed.

Education also has a role in straightening out beliefs by furnishing methods of ascertaining the facts about the social reality, although Myrdal is doubtful about there being a social reality other than our perception of it. Much of the proposed legislation, moreover, makes its claim in the name of consequences that are reasonable or not reasonable to expect. Will a housing project for the poor, for example, lead to the economic improvement of the poor in general? Will an increase in the availability of vocational education for minority youth decrease their unemployment rate? This is the domain of waranted assertion in which information and the use of it in the CAT have their proper place.

The promise of the Myrdal theory of social change lies not so much in the improvement of information so that beliefs become consistent with social reality, however, as in the strain toward a moral consistency. The norms and ideals of the American Creed are the final criteria of social action.

The dominance of the higher-order valuations is the existential pole of the unity; the strain toward consistency with it is the objective, logical pole. This is a possible bridge between truth and credibility; the loyalty to the Creed is the social analogue of sincerity, purity of motive, and authenticity in the assessment of credibility.

Does the American Creed have the credibility that Myrdal ascribed to it in the 1940s? If it does, then utilizing the strain toward social action consistent with it would indeed foster the hope of rational action by the citizenry in a free society. If it does, then debate as to whether particular policies do or do not conform to it would be vigorous, fruitful, and, in the long run, constructive.

Clearly, such a question would not arise if an affirmative answer could be taken for granted. That there is a substantial body of citizens with allegiance to the Creed is beyond question. Even more subscribe to the language of the Creed and use it as justification for their ideologies, although the quasi-sacred documents—the Declaration of Independence, the Constitution, and some of the Supreme Court decisions—do not arouse equal patriotic fervor in all segments of the population.

The 1960s certainly made evident the discrepancy between the Creed and some of the actions of government and other establishments. The 1960s also revealed the degree to which the higher valuations of the Creed were geared to the mores of the white middle-class Anglo-Saxon portions of the population. The latter were therefore unable to see the discrepancies between their beliefs in the social reality and the Creed; the minorities, on their part, saw nothing but the discrepancies, and in this they were joined by cadres of white protestors, especially those on the college campus.

The students were incensed about the Vietnam war and middle-class strictures on drugs, dress, and sex. The younger activist members of the university faculty were also incensed about the war, middle-class mores, and all establishments devoted to their preservation. As intellectuals, they went to great lengths to show that the beliefs about the social reality were the product of historical distortion and that their relationship to middle-class white Anglo-Saxon capitalistic dominance had been concealed by the rhetoric of the American Creed, as well as by misguided historians.

Intellectuals quite properly claim the right in the name of the Creed and their occupation to question anything. One form of this questioning is called "debunking a myth," or "exploding a myth," and it is a fairly standard academic occupation. One takes a doctrine so well accepted that its truth is taken for granted and seeks evidence (historical or scientific or whatever kind one's guild demands) to show that the doctrine is false, a myth. The mythical character of the doctrine is attributed to ignorance or deliberate distortion designed to fool the public. In debunking a myth, the scholar may, of course, create another myth for other debunkers.

Debunking has been practiced on various components of the American Creed and interpretations of it, and not always consistently. Again and again, "evidence" is discovered to show that the *real* motives of American politicians and industrialists were oppression of the masses and exploitation of the workers. Yet the very delight in unmasking the alleged hypocrites is itself an acknowledgment of the ideals and norms of the Creed. It is not the Creed or its values that are being rejected by the debunkers but the claim that certain of their forbears were living up to them. Yet if loyalty to the Creed is itself a myth, why should we decry the hypocrites?

The strength of the Creed may lie in the blend of inconsistencies that allow many interpretations of democracy to find confirmation in it, or it may be owing to something more fundamental and universal. The traits of character that the Creed celebrates are difficult to reject, just as the standard list of the virtues in their general and abstract formulation is hard to reject. It might be argued that they remain constant because they define the human essence in any acceptable sense in which we can speak of such an essence. A creature that did not admire courage above cowardice, freedom above slavery, honesty above corruption, and knowledge above ignorance would be regarded as morally deficient, but a creature that did not understand and feel these differences would be regarded as a nonhuman entity, a robot or some form of lower animal. As noted previously, our debates are not about the virtues in their abstract connotation but rather about the behaviors that at any given period in history shall count as proper instances of them. That is why credibility or warranted commitment on matters of human import always return to the beliefs implied by what Myrdal called the high-order valuations.

Consistency, taken as internal, logical consistency, is liable to the de-moralization of social issues, to the substitution of procedures for substance, excessive formalization, organization, and monetization. That is why the consistency has to be with the Creed or some analogous set of moral principles. And it may be that making the Creed or these principles the pivot of credibility may also simplify the complexity that purely pragmatic calculation engenders. Take, for example, the vexing problem of equalizing educational opportunity. Consider the morass of court decisions, legislation, regulations, and agencies that this problem has spawned.

The simple question for equal educational opportunity is whether or not we really believe that all human beings have a uniform generic nature that it is the obligation of the school to nurture. It is in this sense that we are all created equal is more than *mere* rhetoric. If we believe it, there is a nature that variations in nurture cannot fully eliminate. To measure the obligation of the school by the variations that culture has imposed on different groups instead of by their generic unity denies rather than provides equality of educational opportunity. For credibility, equal opportunity should be taken literally. Once we begin adjusting the curriculum and methods to disadvantages, we are in danger of perpetuating them, especially if the differences claim to be desirable. Much of the credibility of the educational establishment hangs on the degree to which it takes the unity of human nature seriously, and how much it uses cultural differences as a cloak for inequality.

AMERICAN CREED + GENERAL EDUCATION + OPTIMISM

The American Creed, as Myrdal termed it, is a happy historical circumstance that gives the schools a common set of values to which a wide diversity of the population can and does subscribe. It can do so in part because of the ambiguity of its higher-order evaluations, but perhaps even more because its components, taken together, resonate to more fundamental human aspirations. The American story is unique in many ways, however derivative its populations and ideas may have been. In its time it was a *new* continent; the nation did grow out of a revolution; it did have vast frontiers; it did assimilate thousands upon thousands of immigrants who knowingly chose to come to its shores, and, aside from the shameful exception of black slavery, did come willingly. The Creed, therefore, evokes strong sentiments of loyalty and patriotism despite internal bickering and political warfare.

The use of the American Creed by the public school as the criterion to which diversity in policies and politics have to conform *in spirit* could be the unifying base that itself would not shift its ground. This, of course, limits the bounds of criticism and controversy and will offend those who hold that the highest good is to question everything. Intellectually, as I have tried to show, this is quite possible, and, for the academic, imperative—that is his stock in trade. But a public school system is not a university department devoted to specialized scholarship; it cannot, so to speak, keep pulling up the radishes to see if they are growing. Given the commitment inherent and latent in the Creed, the school can devote itself to instruction, with which the future citizen can think clearly, knowingly, and critically within that Creed.

As for the curriculum, once the public school accepts instruction in general education as its primary responsibility, highly validated contents in the symbolic skills and basic concepts of the disciplines can be prescribed in grades K–12, for the total school population. These contents can be graded to meet differences in learning rates and experiential readiness; that much educational research should enable us to do. Furthermore, the skills of the CAT can be incorporated into the curriculum as a test of its cognitive content, and by the end of schooling, every pupil can have had an exposure to the exemplars of the culture in the arts and the sciences.

This, of course, is a highly simplified version of the curriculum, and it has been rejected as being inadequate to the special needs of individual pupils and the exigencies of the times. So project curricula, life adjustment curricula, career curricula, and group therapy curricula have been advocated as meeting the diverse needs of pupils and times. These are responses to urgent pressures and cynicism about the efficacy of general education. There is a constant temptation to construct the curriculum out of immediate needs: sex education, drug education, vocational education, remedial reading, reading of utility bills, reading of want ads. Education by doing is interpreted to mean practicing in schools the everyday tasks of nonschool life.

It is not strange, then, that the more the public school tries to translate its curriculum into life tasks, the lower its credibility becomes. As a scholastic cafeteria, it can never be adequate to the variety of taste and needs that it can be called upon to meet. The attempt to meet complexity with complexity is doomed to failure in a society such as ours. The narrower and more specific the goals of schooling, the lower the flexibility of those who undergo it, and the greater the number of unmet needs. For individual differences are not only numerous in their aggregate, but infinite in their variety from moment to moment.

The proposal to reinstitute a fairly standard but highly sophisticated version of the subject-matter curriculum is now regarded as so reactionary as to be radical. It would take another volume to refute these criticisms in detail, as has been attempted elsewhere.[7] Whether it makes sense depends on the interpretations of the probable demands on the citizenry for vocational, civic, and personal adequacy in a modern society. And one might also take into account the success or claims to success of the alternative curricula tried in American schools in the last two decades. Cogent as these considerations might be, the most important issue is to understand the ways in which schooling is used in life; much of the distaste and distrust for general education come from a misunderstanding of its use.

General education is not simply a bundle of skills and concepts to be memorized nor a set of theoretical principles to be applied to problems of action. General education is the formal study of the arts and sciences explicitly in order that the conceptual structure of the disciplines remains to function interpretively and tacitly. They are the glasses we do not see when we look through them. They are the lenses or stencils that organize reality for our perception and understanding in special ways. We use them by selective forgetting. Every time we make a judgment of relevance or place a problem in its relevant context, we are using the residual schemata of our general studies. The educated mind has a full complement of lenses or stencils and uses them with facility.

The tacit component is not absent from Dewey's CAT. For Dewey, the impulse to thinking that activates the method of intelligence is an awareness of discontinuity, of blocked action. A situation is perceived as problematic if it does not yield to customary remedies, and at that juncture observation, hypothesis, prediction, and verification are instituted as phases in the complete act of thought. At every step of the process the tacit conceptual-imagic resources furnish the intimations of relevance. These tacit resources remain as the operational residues of explicit studies in the subjects that make up general education.

Over a discipline curriculum in general education the personnel of the school could claim a high degree of autonomy and intellectual authority. Such a curriculum makes it possible to assess teaching competence and the more elusive "quality" in education and schooling. Once we move away from this kind of curriculum, such judgments become chaotic. Whether the American body politic is willing to afford the benefits of such a general education to all its people is a political question, and its decision will determine whether or not there is a public that a public school system can serve. The valuational unity of the American Creed and cognitive unity of general education are about the minimal commitments that schooling for an enlightened citizenry in a democracy demands. If we can meet these minima, then as far as the school is concerned, there are grounds for rational optimism.

REFERENCES

1. J.A. Symonds, *The Renaissance in Italy; The Revival of Learning* (New York: Henry Holt, 1883), p. 29. This was part of the rediscovery and enchantment with the ideals of Greek and Roman civilization and literature. Emulating the great figures of the civilization was a form of character training. Cf. H.S. Broudy and John Palmer, *Exemplars of Teaching Method* (Chicago: Rand McNally, 1965), chap. 6.

2. Cf. Werner Jaeger, *Paideia: The Ideals of Greek Culture*, trans. G. Highet (New York: Oxford University Press, 1943–45).

3. Cf. *The Moral Judgment*, ed. Paul W. Taylor (Englewood Cliffs, N.J.: Prentice-Hall, 1964).

4. For a typical effort in mustering interest, study, and development in this area, see the reports on the *Citizen Education Project* conducted by the Research for Better Schools, Inc., Philadephia, 1978. The publication contains good bibliographies of relevant materials in the field. *See* also Brian Crittenden, *Form and Content in Moral Education* (Ontario: Ontario Institute for Studies in Education, 1972).

5. *The Tacit Dimension* (Garden City, N.Y.: Doubleday, 1966).

6. *An American Dilemma* (New York: Harper & Bros., 1944).

7. H.S. Broudy, *The Real World of the Public Schools* (New York: Harcourt Brace Jovanovich, 1972); and Broudy, B.O. Smith, and J.R. Burnett, *Democracy and Excellence in American Secondary Education* (Chicago: Rand McNally, 1964; reprint ed., R.E. Krieger, Huntington, N.Y., 1978).

Epilogue

Not infrequently the citizen who has been the subject of this book is asked and asks himself whether he looks forward to life with optimism or pessimism. Pundits and scholars are eager to help him make up his mind and adjust his expectations. As with other fields of prophecy, the outlooks are mixed.

On the pessimistic side are those who, like Irving Kristol, see in the coming decade a disintegrating international order in which economic growth is hard to achieve and maintain.[1] Much of what has been noted in connection with the randomization of good and evil, the inadequacies of our ability to exploit advanced technology, is also pessimistic in its import. Perhaps the most pessimistic aspect for the future is the tendency of every social change to produce both good and evil consequences at the same time but for different components of the social order. We somehow cannot confine the changes to benign consequences, even when we are able to produce them.

The dialectic of social change also operates on scholars. No sooner are the dismal futures outlined than optimistic visions are produced to assure us that population can be controlled, or that resources for sustaining world populations are not limited; that technology will yet see us through our difficulties—even those that technology has itself created.

Finally, there is no lack of religious cults and cultists who predict the doom and rebirth of the world. Some will even name the day on which they will occur, and all offer the means of coping with the former and enjoying the latter.

The credibility of those who see our planet heading toward increasing misery and those who rely on erudite cooperation, planning, and new technology as grounds for optimism is about the same. Because of the randomization of good and evil Las Vegas is as much a symbol of American life as Wall Street, Washington, and Hollywood.

If there is ground for optimism, it is in the constancy of human nature rather than in shrewd analyses and theories about world conditions, resources, populations, climates, and parliaments. Its powers of imagination will create visions of possibility and horror; its intellectual curiosity will keep trying to understand the world so that some possibilities are realized rather than others. The constancy of our ineluctable respect for persons will mitigate the savagery of Hobbes' state of nature, which is prehuman rather than human. The self that creates the moral law cannot be wholly selfish. If human beings as a species cannot respond to the intrinsic worth of the person, there is no limit to the brutality, cruelty, and inhumanity that can be rationalized in the name of expediency. But they can and do respond in this way.

I do not know just when in the course of history that response became a characteristic of the species, but once it occurred in some human mind, an addition to the human reality was created and forever after confronted men as a possibility. Somehow the possibility became an ideal, a call of conscience, and finally a moral obligation. At that moment it also became an ingredient in the definition of man, of humanity, and a factor in natural selection, and thus a species characteristic.

The notions of human and humane could occur only to a species capable of cogitating about the justification as well as the means for survival. The sociobiologists may have the right scenario for the first time around the evolutionary circuit, but once the brain of man could separate images and concepts from their physical referents, the sociobiologists' account becomes strained, and we have to beware the genetic fallacy. The very ideals and ideas that the sociobiologist has to derive from biological conditions in order to keep the theory coherent have a mode of being that leaves their physical origins behind, so far behind that they can almost—not quite—be forgotten. Certainly the biological structures of man give no answer to the question whether survival is worth the trouble; indeed, they make the question a strange puzzle.

For the second time around, the mind creates out of imagination and thought a reality that traffics in what *might* and what *ought* to be as much, if not more, than what actually exists. The most tough-minded social realist betrays his membership in the human reality when he comments: "This is an imperfect world." This is the abiding ground for optimism. The third and forth and hundredth time around the evolutionary circuit have preserved by natural selection those traits that can best survive in a world created by the mind. To be able to live with oneself also achieves survival value. Whether these existential traits have been built into the genes or are learned anew by each generation, we do not have to decide. There is, one must suppose, a genetic boundary that cultural adaptations cannot transcend—at the moment. The persistence of cancer, birth defects, and dozens of other conditions are witness to these boundaries. But these limits are not fixed, and there is reason to believe that in many directions we can go a long way in coping with hostile environments before the boundaries are reached.

This impressionistic sketch of the evolution of human nature is a far cry from the Aristotelian notion that in the human being there is a *telos,* an end, an ideal form which it strives to actualize. And yet even if this ideal or form or *telos* is itself the product of human imagination and thought, and even though it achieves species status only after a long evolution, its power as a regulative ideal of reason is nonetheless real. The search for the unity of mankind has to begin with it; only then can it proceed humanely to more concrete social arrangements. The concept of human nature limits the fragmentation of a society consisting of individual selves, not by the sacrifice of selfhood, but rather by an ultimate respect for it.

In the end, our optimism and pessimism depend as much on the reality we as human beings create as on the reality we find. The human impulse to free our knowledge from the personal and subjective distortion is appropriate to our probing of all reality, found or imagined; this is our intellectual categorical imperative. Its propositions are true or false whether we like it or not. Yet objective truth becomes impotent by the very independence it achieves from persons. To regain potency, knowledge must rejoin human purpose. And once purpose becomes active, the motives of the actors become relevant and truth regains a moral dimension. The greater the amount of technical expert knowledge that is available, the greater the dependence of the citizen on the credibility of witnesses—on their moral integrity, their candor, their willingness to live by the truths they proclaim. Whether the deliverances of the professions, professors, and bureaucrats will help the citizen to act rationally depends on whether by their commitment they can establish credibility.

The school is no exception. It too has to establish grounds for credibility; some of these grounds it borrows from the guilds of the learned and the wise, some from the commitments of the community to the common good, and some from its own expertise. All of these borrowings will fail if the school's own commitment to its mission, its compact with society, is open to doubt.

REFERENCE

1. *Wall Street Journal*, 26 November 1979.

Index